# Vietnamese
## Cooking

Over 60 step-by-step recipes in 250 stunning photographs

Ghillie Başan

with photography by Martin Brigdale

southwater

This edition is published by Southwater, an imprint of Anness Publishing Ltd Hermes House, 88–89 Blackfriars Road, London SE1 8HA tel. 020 7401 2077; fax 020 7633 9499 www.southwaterbooks.com; www.annesspublishing.com

If you would like to investigate using the images in this book for publishing, promotions or advertising, please visit our website www.practicalpictures.com for more information.

UK agent: The Manning Partnership Ltd, 6 The Old Dairy, Melcombe Road, Bath BA2 3LR; tel. 01225 478444; fax 01225 478440; sales@manning-partnership.co.uk

UK distributor: Grantham Book Services Ltd, Isaac Newton Way, Alma Park Industrial Estate, Grantham, Lincs NG31 9SD; tel. 01476 541080; fax 01476 541061; orders@gbs.tbs-ltd.co.uk

North American agent/distributor: National Book Network, 4501 Forbes Boulevard, Suite 200, Lanham, MD 20706; tel. 301 459 3366; fax 301 429 5746; www.nbnbooks.com

Australian agent/distributor: Pan Macmillan Australia, Level 18, St Martins Tower, 31 Market St, Sydney, NSW 2000; tel. 1300 135 113; fax 1300 135 103; customer.service@macmillan.com.au

New Zealand agent/distributor: David Bateman Ltd, 30 Tarndale Grove, Off Bush Road, Albany, Auckland; tel. (09) 415 7664; fax (09) 415 8892

Publisher: Joanna Lorenz
Senior Managing Editor: Conor Kilgallon
Project Editors: Doreen Gillon, Emma Clegg and Molly Perham
Photographer: Martin Brigdale
Home economists: Lucy McKelvie and Bridget Sargeson
Stylist: Helen Trent
Designer: Nigel Partridge
Cover Design: Anthony Cohen
Production Controller: Lee Sargent

ETHICAL TRADING POLICY
At Anness Publishing we believe that business should be conducted in an ethical and ecologically sustainable way, with respect for the environment and a proper regard to the replacement of the natural resources we employ.

As a publisher, we use a lot of wood pulp to make high-quality paper for printing, and that wood commonly comes from spruce trees. We are therefore currently growing more than 500,000 trees in two Scottish forest plantations near Aberdeen – Berrymoss (130 hectares/320 acres) and West Touxhill (125 hectares/305 acres). The forests we manage contain twice the number of trees employed each year in paper-making for our books.

Because of this ecological investment programme, you can have the reassurance of knowing that a tree is being cultivated on your behalf to naturally replace the materials used to make the book you are holding.

Our forestry programme is run in accordance with the UK Woodland Assurance Scheme (UKWAS) and will be certified by the internationally recognized Forest Stewardship Council (FSC). The FSC is a non-government organization dedicated to promoting responsible management of the world's forests. Certification ensures forests are managed in an environmentally sustainable and socially responsible basis. For further information about this scheme, go to www.annesspublishing.com/trees

1 3 5 7 9 10 8 6 4 2

Previously published as part of a larger volume, The Food and Cooking of Vietnam & Cambodia.

Main cover image shows Stir-fried Pork with Peanuts, Lime and Basil from page 47.

NOTES
Bracketed terms are intended for American readers. For all recipes, quantities are given in both metric and imperial measures and, where appropriate, in standard cups and spoons. Follow one set of measures, but not a mixture.

Standard spoon and cup measures are level. 1 tsp = 5ml, 1 tbsp = 15ml, 1 cup = 250ml/ 8fl oz. Australian standard tablespoons are 20ml. Australian readers should use 3 tsp in place of 1 tbsp for measuring small quantities. American pints are 16fl oz/ 2 cups. American readers should use 20fl oz/ 2.5 cups in place of 1 pint when measuring liquids.

Electric oven temperatures in this book are for conventional ovens. When using a fan oven, the temperature will probably need to be reduced by about 10–20°C/ 20–40°F. Since ovens vary, you should check with your manufacturer's instruction book for guidance.

The nutritional analysis given for each recipe is calculated per portion (i.e. serving or item), unless otherwise stated. If the recipe gives a range, such as Serves 4–6, then the nutritional analysis will be for the smaller portion size, i.e. 6 servings. Measurements for sodium do not include salt added to taste.

Medium (US large) eggs are used unless otherwise stated.

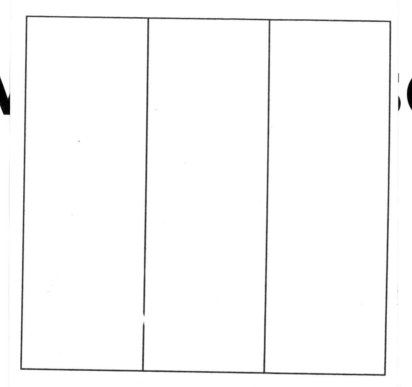

# CONTENTS

# VIETNAM TODAY

Today Vietnam is a thrilling place to be. Resplendent with colour, exotic smells, and delicious tastes, it has risen from the ruins with its spirit intact. From the border with China in the north to the rice mills of the Mekong Delta in the south, this land of rivers and lush, emerald-green paddy fields hums with activity. There are unspoiled beaches, peaceful lagoons, dense jungles and rugged mountains with roaring waterfalls. Visitors are graciously accepted and the Vietnamese people, in spite of their history of hardship and suffering, are always smiling and friendly.

Since the opening of Vietnam to tourism, there has been a new wave of excitement in all aspects of its culture, with a growing emphasis on the cuisine. And, with the spread of Vietnamese refugees to different corners of the world, authentic restaurants have mushroomed in Sydney, Paris and California, all presenting an intriguing fusion of flavours and history.

*Below: The floating market at the village of Phung Help, in the Mekong Delta.*

The Vietnamese are keen snackers. Life is generally lived in the streets so wherever you go there are markets, small restaurants, cafés and makeshift stalls made out of bamboo, selling or cooking every type of snack. The southern city of Ho Chi Minh City is abuzz with the sounds and sights of culinary activity. The streets are so enticingly thick with the smell of cooking you could almost bite the air. From the minute the city awakens just before dawn, the tables and stools are ready for early workers who come to slurp their bowls of the classic noodles soup *pho*. Other people sit waiting for the slow drip of coffee filtering into cups. Pungent spices like cinnamon, ginger and star anise tickle your nose as you walk about among the chaos of sputtering motorbikes, pedestrians dodging traffic, tinkling bicycles with ducks and hens spilling out of baskets and fruit sellers weaving their way through the crowds, pushing carts of pineapple, mango or papaya, freshly peeled and kept cool on a bed of ice. You don't have to look for food in Vietnam; it finds you!

*Above: Preparing food at a market stall in Hoi An.*

## MARKETS

Along the Mekong Delta, some markets are on boats. The best known is the floating market Cai Ran, where the boats converge at dawn. It is a colourful sight as boats laden with bright green bitter melons, long, white radishes, scarlet tomatoes, yellow fruits and freshly cut herbs, bob peacefully in the water.

The countryside village markets are more reminiscent of a busy barnyard. The squawking and cackling of hens and ducks, and other forms of livestock, remind you that one striking fact about the Vietnamese is that there is little they don't eat. Roasted dog's head, stir-fried ducks' tongues, grilled field rats, monkey roasted on a spit or the heart of a venomous snake are all part of the daily fare. In these live markets, you will also find fish bladders, cockerels' testicles, crunchy insects, bats, toads, sparrows and turtle doves, crocodiles, armadillos, bears and sea horses.

## GEOGRAPHICAL INFLUENCES

Vietnam has often been described as a "pearl necklace" perched on the edge of Indochina. The Mekong branches out into the South China Sea below Ho Chi Minh City and serves as a highway for boat traffic and trade. Its source is a stream in the Tibetan Himalayas, from where it tumbles down through steep gorges in south-western China, through the jungles of Laos and Cambodia until it flows at a leisurely pace through the lush pastures of southern Vietnam.

As the Vietnamese will point out, their country is shaped like a *don ganh*, the traditional bamboo pole that is slung over the shoulder with a basket of rice hanging from each end. These baskets represent the rice bowls of Vietnam, the Red River Delta in the north and the Mekong Delta in the south, joined by a mountainous spine. A long coastline and the numerous flowing rivers and streams that carve up the land, provide Vietnam with such a volume of water that it has a steady supply of its two most important ingredients: rice and *nuoc mam*, the fermented fish sauce.

### The north

In the mountainous region of northern Vietnam there is still a large Chinese population, and the emphasis of the cuisine is on contrasting flavours and textures within the meal. The food is milder than the spicy dishes of the south, relying on mild black pepper and the indigenous herbs, which include basil, mint and coriander (cilantro).

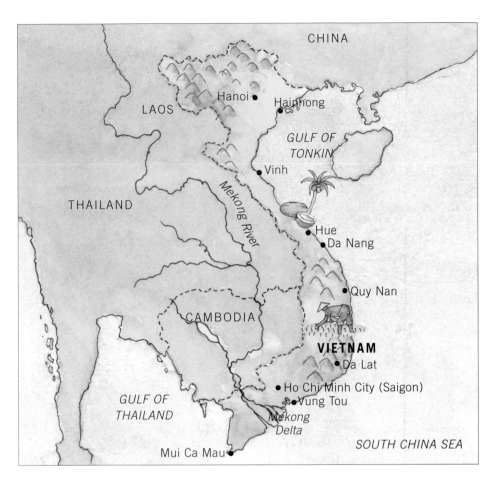

Hanoi, the principal city in the north, is reputed for its rice rolls, sweet snacks made with mung beans, and its snail dishes. The communal dish *lau*, which is often translated as "hotpot" but is in fact more akin to the French meat fondue, is attributed to the north, as is the favourite noodle soup, *pho*.

### Hue

Of all the cities in Vietnam, there is none so representative of culture and learning as the historic, garden city of Hue. Once the imperial city, Hue was considered the centre of *haute cuisine*. The emperor Tu Duc, who reigned from 1848 to 1883, demanded ingenuity from his kitchens to create a refined cuisine. To achieve this, he expected 50 dishes to be prepared by 50 cooks and served by 50 servants at each meal. In Hue today, service remains formal and food is still presented in many small bowls as if feeding the emperor. Here you might find crab claws stuffed with pork, beef wrapped in wild betel leaves, and minced prawns wrapped around sugar cane (*chao tom*). A variety of crops are grown in this part of Vietnam, such as aubergines (eggplants), bitter melons, pumpkins, mangoes, pineapples and artichokes. Game birds, river fish and seafood are in abundant supply.

### Ho Chi Minh City

The southern region of Vietnam is characterized by Ho Chi Minh City, formerly Saigon. At one time the languid Paris of the Orient, it is the centre of commerce and trade. The food relies heavily on the rice bowl and growing pastures of the Mekong Delta, and most produce comes from around Dalat. Just about anything grows here, including avocados, white strawberries, peaches, cauliflowers, tomatoes, tropical fruits and salad vegetables, all of which are incorporated in the region's dishes, which are served with French bread almost as often as with rice or noodles. Coconuts and sugar cane provide the base ingredients for many dishes.

# CUSTOMS & FESTIVALS

As eating plays such an important role in Vietnamese society, there are certain requirements of dining etiquette, although this can vary from region to region. For example, in northern and central Vietnam, it is custom for the oldest family member to sit nearest the door and everyone else to be arranged in descending age. The eldest will also be the first to help himself to food and a host will often serve the guest. In the south where the traditions of etiquette are more relaxed, everyone can dive in and help themselves. If you are the guest, one tradition that is important to remember is the bearing of a small gift. Whether you are invited to eat in a home or restaurant, throughout Asia, from Turkey to China, it is polite to bring your hosts a little box of something sweet or a bunch of fresh flowers – although in Vietnam the flowers should never be white as this signifies death.

## COMMUNAL DINING

As with most Asian countries, dining is a communal affair. A selection of dishes may be put on a table and each diner will be given their own individual bowl into which the food is spooned. When passing the food around, two hands are used to hold the dish and the exchange is acknowledged with a nod. Food is usually eaten with fingers, chopsticks or

*Below: Delicate lotus flowers are used to decorate tables and plates of food.*

spoons, although the Vietnamese have a knack of sipping their food from the spoons without ever putting the spoon into their mouths.

The proper way to eat is to take some rice from the communal dish and put it in your bowl, then use the ceramic spoon to transfer the meat, fish or vegetables onto your rice. Hold the bowl up near to your mouth and use the chopsticks to shovel in the tasty morsels. It is polite for the host to offer more food than the guests can eat but, equally, it is polite for the guests not to eat everything in sight.

Depending on the complexity of the meal, there will be a number of individual dipping bowls, containing sweet or spicy condiments, and there may also be bowls of chillies or pickled vegetables to crunch and chew on between mouthfuls. When the Vietnamese eat, there is a great deal of gutsy enjoyment and noisy slurping. Eating is almost a game – there are crabs to crack, prawns to suck, food to be wrapped and rolled, and a lot of mess as they love lingering over food.

*Above: A vendor selling the pungent fruit durian and other local fruits in Ho Chi Minh City.*

## FAMILY CELEBRATIONS

For the Vietnamese, to show a "big face" is a sign of prestige. Weddings and family celebrations are often elaborate and ruinously expensive for some families, but the cost is less important than "losing" face. A great deal of preparation goes into these events so that the food is overflowing. Each celebration calls for traditional, time-consuming specialities, and opulent dishes will appear, such as the Vietnamese roast duck, sliced into juicy slabs, drizzled with the piquant fish sauce (*nuoc cham*), and wrapped in lettuce leaves; sticky rice cakes steamed in lotus leaves and decorated with lotus flowers; and highly prized whole fish, grilled (broiled) or steamed with the head presented to the guest who is destined for good fortune. On these occasions, the habitual fragrant tea may be cast aside for a little merriment with beer and wine.

## RELIGIOUS FESTIVALS

Vietnam's calendar is full of festivals, all of which call for elaborate feasting and celebration. The national celebrations include Liberation Day, which marks the date that Saigon surrendered; National Day on 2 September, to mark the Declaration of Independence of the Democratic Republic of Vietnam by Ho Chi Minh in 1945; and Ho Chi Minh's Birthday.

The religious festivals take place according to the lunar calendar, so the dates change from year to year. Important religious festivals include Buddha's Birthday, *Phat Dan*; Christmas; the Holiday of the Dead, *Thanh Minh*, when people visit the graves of dead relatives to light incense and make offerings of food and flowers; Wandering Souls Day, when offerings of food and gifts are made for the forgotten dead; and the mid-Autumn Festival, which lands on the fifteenth day of the eighth moon. To celebrate the harvest, children take part in an evening procession, holding colourful lanterns in the form of dragons, fish, boats and unicorns, while the drums and cymbals play and festive snacks and sweets, such as sticky rice cakes filled with lotus seeds, peanuts, and candied watermelon seeds, are sold in the streets.

### Tet – Vietnamese New Year

*Tet Nguyen Dan*, meaning "New Dawn", is the most important festival of the Vietnamese lunar year. It falls some time between mid-January and mid-February and lasts for three days. It is a time of renewing and reaffirming beliefs in life, love, family and community. Families reunite in the hope of success and prosperity in the coming year. Cemeteries are visited and the spirits of dead relatives are invited home for the *Tet* celebrations. Homes and graves are cleaned and decorations are put up. The rites for *Tet* begin a week in advance.

The first rite is the ascension of the Spirits of the Hearth to the heavens. These kitchen gods dwell in every kitchen and must ride on the backs of fish to report on the year's events to the Jade Emperor in the hope of bringing

back good luck for the family. To aid them on their journey, families all over Vietnam put live carp into the rivers and lakes and leave offerings of food and fresh water at the altars. At the stroke of midnight on New Year's Eve, the noise of drums and cymbals mark the beginning of the celebrations as the gods are welcomed back.

The first meal of *Tet* is one for the ancestors as they are believed to have returned to the world of the living. The head of the family will offer a grace, light three incense sticks, then invite five generations of the deceased, whispering their names, to join in the family feast. This ceremony of "ancestor calling" takes place at the morning and evening meals for the three days of *Tet*. The second day of *Tet* involves visiting the wife's family and close friends and the third day is for embracing the community. Families visit the school teachers, patients visit their doctors, and many people visit astrologers to hear the year's fortunes. On the evening of the third day, the ancestors depart.

The principal *Tet* speciality is *banh chung*, sticky rice cakes filled with bean paste and, traditionally, wrapped in a green *dong* (similar to a banana leaf) parcel and tied with bamboo twine. Throughout the festivities, stacks of *banh chung* are piled high in the stalls next to watermelons and dragon fruit,

*Above: Street vendors selling sweet snacks and fruit.*

sweets, lotus seeds dyed a festive red to represent joy, truth and sincerity, and the popular *mut*, a candied concoction of vegetables and dried fruits, which are on display among the woven, painted masks. Lucky money is placed on trees as offerings to the ancestors and homes are decorated with trees, such as pretty, fruit-laden kumquats, or peach and apricot trees, resplendent in perfumed blossom, to ward off evil spirits.

*Below: Traditional dancers performing in Hue, Vietnam.*

# COOKING EQUIPMENT

The traditional Vietnamese kitchen is basic. Often dark and sparsely kitted out with an open hearth, very little equipment is needed. Food is generally bought daily from the markets, taken home and cooked immediately so, unless you visit the kitchen during the frenzied moments of passionate activity over the hearth, there is little evidence of food or cooking. Without refrigerators, this reliance on fresh produce from the daily markets is vital. For some, two visits to the market are required – in the morning for the ingredients to cook for lunch, and, in the afternoon for the evening meal. Back in the simple kitchen, the activity always begins with the scrubbing of vegetables, the plucking and jointing of birds (if this hasn't been done in the markets), the endless chopping and slicing, and the pounding of herbs and spices with a pestle and mortar.

## WOK

The wok is the most important utensil for everyday cooking in Vietnam. Everybody has one. Without a doubt, there is always something delicious being stir-fried in a home or in the streets. However, woks are not only used for stir-frying, they are also used for steaming, deep-frying, braising and soup-making. The most functional, multi-purpose wok should measure approximately 35cm/14in across, large enough for a family meal or to steam a whole fish. The most common wok is double-handled and made of lightweight carbonized steel. This is ideal for deep-frying and steaming but, for stir-frying, you need the single-handled version.

When you first buy a wok, you need to season it before use. Put it over a high heat to blacken the inside – this burns off any dust and factory coating. Leave the wok to cool, then immerse it in hot, soapy water and clean it with an abrasive cloth or stiff brush. Rinse it well and dry over a medium heat. Pour a little cooking oil into the base and, using a piece of kitchen paper, wipe it all around the surface of the wok. Now the wok is ready for use.

After each use, clean the wok with hot water only, dry it over a medium heat, and wipe a thin layer of oil over the surface. This will ensure that it doesn't get rusty. Over time, the wok

*Above: A solid mortar and pestle is an essential piece of kitchen equipment.*

will acquire a seasoned look – dark and glossy – and should last a lifetime. Woks are sold in all Chinese and Asian markets.

### MORTAR AND PESTLE

A big mortar and pestle, made of stone, is of particular value, as it is used not only for grinding spices, chillies and garlic, but also for pounding all the condiments and pastes, as well as the meat for pâtés and savoury balls. Some cooks have several mortar and pestle sets, varying in size according to the activity and ingredient. Coffee grinders and electric blenders can be used as substitutes, but they don't release the oils and flavours of the ingredients in the same way and they produce too smooth a texture. It is worth looking for a solid stone mortar and pestle in Asian markets and kitchen suppliers.

### BAMBOO STEAMER

Traditional bamboo steamers come in various sizes. The most practical one is about 30cm/12in wide, as it can be used for rice or a whole fish. Generally, the steamer is set directly over a wok that is filled with boiling water to below the level of the steamer. The food is placed in the steamer, either on a plate, or wrapped in muslin (cheesecloth), or banana leaves. The lid is placed on the steamer and, as the water in the wok is heated, the steam rises under and around the food, cooking it gently. A stainless steel steamer is no substitute

*Left: A single-handed wok is good for stir-frying on the hob.*

for a bamboo one, which imparts its own delicate fragrance to the dish. Bamboo steamers are available in most Asian stores and some cooking equipment suppliers.

## CHOPSTICKS

In Vietnam, chopsticks are used routinely to eat with, as well as being used for cooking. Following Chinese methods many Vietnamese cooks tend to use a set of long chopsticks for stirring, mixing, tasting, and also as tongs. Eating chopsticks are traditionally made from bamboo or wood, but more elaborate ones are often made from ivory, bone, gold, silver or jade. For cooking, look for long chopsticks made from bamboo.

## CLAY POT

Made from a combination of light-coloured clay and sand, these pots come in all sizes,

*Above: A clay pot can be used in the oven or, with care, on the stove.*

*Right: A medium-weight cleaver is a multi-purpose tool.*

*Right: Bamboo steamers come in several sizes.*

with single or double handles, lids, and glazed interiors. Perhaps the oldest form of cooking vessel, these attractive pots are ideal for slow-cooking, such as braised dishes and soups, as they retain an overall even heat. Generally, they are used on the stove over a low or medium heat, as a high temperature could cause them to crack. When you first buy a clay pot, it needs to be treated for cooking. Fill it with water and place it over a low flame. Gradually increase the heat and let the water boil until it is reduced by half. Rinse the pot and dry thoroughly. Now it is ready for use. Traditional clay pots are available in some Asian markets.

*Left: Bamboo chopsticks are essential kitchen equipment.*

## CLEAVERS

Asian cleavers are the most important tools in the kitchen. There are special blades for the fine chopping of lemon grass and green papaya, heavy blades for opening coconuts, thin ones for shredding spring onions (scallions), and multi-purpose ones for any type of chopping, slicing and crushing. Generally, you use the front, lighter part of the blade for the regular chopping, slicing and shredding; the back, heavier section is for chopping with force through bones; and the flat side is ideal for crushing ginger and garlic, and for transporting the ingredients into the wok.

## DRAINING SPOON

Traditional draining spoons are made of wire with a long bamboo handle; more modern ones are made of perforated stainless steel. Both are flat and extremely useful for deep-frying, for blanching noodles and for scooping ingredients out of hot liquid.

*Right: Draining spoons are useful for deep-frying and blanching.*

# COOKING TECHNIQUES

The traditional cooking methods of Vietnam require few culinary tools but do need a great deal of attention to detail. Fresh ingredients are of the utmost importance, followed by the balance of sharp or mild, salty or sweet, bitter or sour, or a combination of all of these flavours. The layering of ingredients is also important, especially in Vietnamese noodle dishes, where flavours and textures should complement each other but remain separate. Almost every meal is prepared from scratch, starting with the plucking of chickens and grinding of spices, followed by the grilling over charcoal, gentle simmering and steaming, or stir-frying. Armed with the correct equipment, the cooking is fairly easy – most of the work is in the preparation.

### Grinding and pounding
Spices, herbs and other ingredients are usually ground and pounded in a large, heavy mortar made of stone. The interior of the mortar should be rough to grip the ingredients and act as an abrasive. The pestle needs to be heavy too, made of the same stone, to provide the right weight for pounding and grinding.

Grinding is most efficient if the herbs, spices and other ingredients are added in the correct order. First the hard seeds or nuts are ground together, then the fresh herbs, ginger and garlic, followed by the oils or pastes. The mixture is then bound and seasoned and ready for use.

## DRY-FRYING

Dried spices are often roasted before grinding to release their natural oils and enhance the aroma. This is done by spreading the spices thinly in a heavy frying pan and putting it over a high heat. As the pan begins to heat, shake it so that the spices don't get too brown. Once the spices begin to colour and their aroma fills the air, put them in a mortar and grind to a powder.

## BRAISING

The classic method for slow-cooked dishes is braising. Generally, oily fish, duck and red meat are cooked this way, often with pungent herbs, spices and coconut milk or juice. Traditionally, to seal in the moisture, a covered clay pot is used as the cooking vessel. Placed over a medium heat, or in the oven, the cooking process can take anything from 30 minutes to 2 hours, depending on the dish. If you don't have a clay pot, use a heavy-based casserole. The key is in containing the moisture and even heat distribution, so don't use a thin aluminium pot.

1 Put all the ingredients in a clay pot and place in a preheated oven. (It can also be placed over a medium heat on the stove if you prefer.)

## GRILLING OVER CHARCOAL

As conventional grills (broilers) don't exist in the majority of homes in Vietnam, grilling is generally done over hot charcoal. This traditional method of cooking not only lends itself to many types of food, it also enhances the taste. Whole fish, pigs or chickens can be cooked this way. Tasty, marinated morsels of food, skewered on bamboo sticks and grilled in the streets, make popular snacks. When cooking over charcoal, light the coals and wait until they have turned red with grey or white ashes. If the charcoal is too hot, the food will just burn.

### Wooden and bamboo skewers
If you are using wooden or bamboo skewers, soak them in water for about 30 minutes before using to prevent them from burning.

## STEAMING

This is a popular way of preparing delicate-tasting foods, such as fish and shellfish, the French-inspired pork pâtés, and sticky rice cakes wrapped in banana or bamboo leaves. Place the food in a bamboo steamer, which should be lined with leaves if the food isn't wrapped in them. Put the lid on the steamer and set it over a wok that is half-filled with water. Bring the water to the boil, then reduce the heat and steam the food according to the recipe.

## STIR-FRYING

Of all the cooking techniques, this is the most important one in Vietnam. The technique is more in the preparation of ingredients than in the cooking process, which only takes minutes. Generally, the ingredients should be cut or shredded into bitesize morsels and laid out in the order in which they are to be cooked. To stir-fry successfully you need a wok, placed over a high heat, and a ladle or spatula to toss the ingredients around, so that they cook but still retain their freshness and crunchy texture.

**1** Pour a little oil into the wok and place it over a high heat until hot.

**2** Add the spices and aromatics to the oil – it should sizzle on contact – and toss them around to flavour the oil.

**3** Add the pieces of meat or fish, and toss them around the wok for a minute or two.

**4** Add the sliced or shredded root vegetables or mushrooms and stir-fry for a minute.

**5** Add the leafy vegetables or bean-sprouts and toss them around quickly.

**6** Finally, toss in the herbs and seasonings and serve immediately. The key is to work quickly and layer the ingredients according to the length of time they require for cooking. Serve hot straight from the wok into warmed bowls and don't leave the food sitting in the wok.

## DEEP-FRYING

Use an oil that can be heated to a high temperature, such as groundnut (peanut) oil, and don't put in too much cold food at once, as this will cool the oil down.

**1** Pour the oil into a pan or wok (filling it no more than two-thirds full) and heat to about 180°C/350°F. To test the temperature, add a drop of batter or a piece of onion. If it sinks, the oil is not hot enough; if it burns, it is too hot. If it sizzles and rises to the surface, the temperature is perfect.

**2** Cook the food in small batches until crisp and lift out with a slotted spoon or wire mesh skimmer when cooked. Drain on a wire rack lined with kitchen paper and serve immediately, or keep warm in the oven until ready to serve.

## BLANCHING

This method is often used to cook delicate meat such as chicken breast portions or duck.

**1** Place the meat and any flavourings in a pan and add just enough water to cover. Bring to the boil, then remove from the heat and leave to stand, covered, for 10 minutes, then drain.

# SOUPS & SAVOURY SNACKS

*Snacks are an important part of the Vietnamese diet. Life is busy on the streets, and wherever you go there are small restaurants, cafés and makeshift stalls made out of bamboo, selling every type of savoury bite. Soups and broths are also served as snacks, and as appetizers and accompaniments to steamed rice. Savoury treats such as Deep-fried Sweet Potato Patties and soups such as Sour Broth with Water Spinach and Beef will ensure your first taste of Vietnam is truly memorable.*

# VIETNAMESE SPRING ROLLS

*ONE OF THE MOST POPULAR FOODS THROUGHOUT VIETNAM IS THE SPRING ROLL, WHICH MAKES AN IDEAL QUICK SNACK. THEY ARE CALLED CHA GIO IN THE SOUTH AND NEM RAN IN THE NORTH, AND THEIR FILLINGS VARY FROM REGION TO REGION.*

**3** Have ready a damp dishtowel, some clear film (plastic wrap) and a bowl of water. Dip a rice wrapper in the water and place it on the damp towel. Spoon about 15ml/1 tbsp of the spring roll filling on to the side nearest to you, just in from the edge. Fold the nearest edge over the filling, fold over the sides, tucking them in neatly, and then roll the whole wrapper into a tight cylinder. Place the roll on a plate and cover with clear film to keep it moist. Continue making spring rolls in the same way, using the remaining wrappers and filling.

MAKES ABOUT 30

INGREDIENTS
    30 dried rice wrappers
    vegetable oil, for deep-frying
    1 bunch fresh mint, stalks removed,
        and *nuoc cham*, to serve
For the filling
    50g/2oz dried bean thread
        (cellophane) noodles, soaked in
        warm water for 20 minutes
    25g/1oz dried cloud ear (wood ear)
        mushrooms, soaked in warm water
        for 15 minutes
    2 eggs
    30ml/2 tbsp *nuoc mam*
    2 garlic cloves, crushed
    10ml/2 tsp sugar
    1 onion, finely chopped
    3 spring onions (scallions), sliced
    350g/12oz/1½ cups minced
        (ground) pork
    175g/6oz/1¾ cups cooked crab meat
        or raw prawns (shrimp)
    salt and ground black pepper

**1** To make the filling, squeeze dry the soaked noodles and chop them into small pieces. Squeeze dry the soaked dried cloud ear mushrooms and chop them.

**2** Beat the eggs in a bowl. Stir in the *nuoc mam*, garlic and sugar. Add the onion, spring onions, noodles, mushrooms, pork and crab meat or prawns. Season well with salt and ground black pepper.

**COOK'S TIP**
These spring rolls filled with rice noodles are typically Vietnamese, but you can substitute beansprouts for the noodles to create rolls more akin to the Chinese version. Fresh mint leaves give these rolls a refreshing bite, but fresh coriander (cilantro), basil or flatleaf parsley work just as well and give an interesting flavour. Dipped into a piquant sauce of your choice, they are very moreish.

**4** Heat the vegetable oil in a wok or heavy pan for deep-frying. Make sure it is hot enough by dropping in a small piece of bread; it should foam and sizzle. Cook the spring rolls in batches, turning them in the oil so that they become golden all over. Drain them on kitchen paper and serve immediately with mint leaves to wrap around them and *nuoc cham* for dipping.

Per portion Energy 63Kcal/236kJ; Protein 2g; Carbohydrate 5g, of which sugars 1g; Fat 4g, of which saturates 1g; Cholesterol 20mg; Calcium 10mg; Fibre 0.3g; Sodium 60mg

# DEEP-FRIED SWEET POTATO PATTIES

*THIS DISH, BANH TOM, IS A HANOI SPECIALITY. THE STREET SELLERS IN THE CITY AND THE CAFÉS ALONG THE BANKS OF WEST LAKE ARE WELL KNOWN FOR THEIR VARIED AND DELICIOUS BANH TOM. TRADITIONALLY, THE PATTIES ARE SERVED WITH HERBS AND LETTUCE LEAVES FOR WRAPPING.*

### SERVES FOUR

INGREDIENTS

50g/2oz/½ cup plain
  (all-purpose) flour
50g/2oz/½ cup rice flour
4ml/scant 1 tsp baking powder
10ml/2 tsp sugar
2.5cm/1in fresh root ginger,
  peeled and grated
2 spring onions (scallions),
  finely sliced
175g/6oz small fresh prawns
  (shrimp), peeled and deveined
1 slim sweet potato, about
  225g/8oz, peeled and cut into
  fine matchsticks
vegetable oil, for deep-frying
salt and ground black pepper
chopped fresh coriander (cilantro),
  to garnish
lettuce leaves *and nuoc cham* or
  other dipping sauce, to serve

**1** Sift the plain and rice flour and baking powder into a bowl. Add the sugar and about 2.5ml/½ tsp each of salt and pepper. Gradually stir in 250ml/8fl oz/1 cup water, until thoroughly combined. Add the grated ginger and sliced spring onions and leave to stand for 30 minutes. Add extra ginger if you like a strong flavour.

**COOK'S TIP**

*Banh tom* made with sweet potato are particularly popular in Hanoi, but they are also very good made with strips of winter melon or courgette (zucchini), beansprouts or bamboo shoots, or finely sliced cabbage leaves. Simply replace the sweet potato with the vegetable of your choice, add a little chilli, if you like, shape into patties and cook as before. You can make the patties any size: small for a snack or first course, or large for a main course; simply adjust the amount you spoon on to the spatula before frying. Serve the patties with a piquant or tangy dipping sauce of your own choice.

**2** Add the prawns and sweet potato to the batter and fold them in, making sure they are well coated. Heat enough oil for deep-frying in a wok. Place a heaped tablespoon of the mixture on to a metal spatula. Lower it into the oil, pushing it off the spatula so that it floats in the oil. Fry for 2–3 minutes, turning it over so that it is evenly browned. Drain on kitchen paper. Continue with the rest of the batter, frying the patties in batches.

**3** Arrange the patties on lettuce leaves, garnish with coriander, and serve immediately with *nuoc cham* or another dipping sauce of your choice.

**Per portion** Energy 276Kcal/1159kJ; Protein 11g; Carbohydrate 35g, of which sugars 6g; Fat 11g, of which saturates 1g; Cholesterol 85mg; Calcium 83mg; Fibre 81g; Sodium 200mg

# GRILLED SHRIMP PASTE ON SUGAR CANE SKEWERS

*THIS DISH, KNOWN AS CHAO TOM IN VIETNAM, IS A CLASSIC. ORIGINALLY CREATED BY THE INGENIOUS COOKS OF THE IMPERIAL KITCHENS IN HUE, IT HAS BECOME A NATIONAL TREASURE. TO APPRECIATE ITS FULL IMPACT, IT IS BETTER TO SIMPLY GRILL IT AND EAT IT BY ITSELF, ENJOYING EVERY SINGLE BITE, RIGHT DOWN TO THE SWEET, SMOKY FLAVOURS OF THE SUGAR CANE.*

SERVES FOUR

INGREDIENTS

50g/2oz pork fat
7.5ml/1½ tsp vegetable oil
1 onion, finely chopped
2 garlic cloves, crushed
1 egg
15ml/1 tbsp fish sauce
15ml/1 tbsp raw cane or
  dark brown sugar
15ml/1 tbsp cornflour (cornstarch)
350g/12oz raw prawns (shrimp),
  peeled and deveined
a piece of fresh sugar cane,
  about 20cm/8in long
salt and ground black pepper

**1** Place the pork fat in a large pan of boiling water and boil for 2–3 minutes. Drain well and chop using a sharp knife. Set aside.

**COOK'S TIP**
Although canned sugar cane can be used for this recipe, it is no substitute for fresh. Fresh sugar cane is often available in African, Caribbean and Asian markets, as well as in some supermarkets. When cooked in the Vietnamese home, this dish is usually served with the traditional accompaniments of salad, rice wrappers and a dipping sauce. The grilled shrimp paste is pulled off the sugar cane, wrapped in a rice paper and dipped in sauce. The stripped sugar cane can then be chewed.

**2** Heat the oil in a heavy pan and stir in the onion and garlic. Just as they begin to colour, remove from the heat and transfer them to a bowl. Beat in the egg, fish sauce and sugar, until the sugar has dissolved. Season with a little salt and plenty of black pepper, and then stir in the cornflour.

**3** Add the pork fat and prawns to the mixture, and mix well. Grind in a mortar using a pestle, or process to a slightly lumpy paste in a food processor.

**VARIATION**
At home, this dish makes a fascinating appetizer or an interesting addition to a barbecue spread. To savour the wonderful tastes, it is best served by itself, straight from the hot grill. There is nothing quite like it!

**4** Divide the paste into eight portions. Using a strong knife or cleaver, cut the sugar cane in half and then cut each half into quarters lengthways. Take a piece of sugar cane in your hand and mould a portion of the paste around it, pressing it gently so the edges are sealed. Place the coated sticks on an oiled tray, while you make the remaining skewers in the same way.

**5** For the best flavour, cook the shrimp paste skewers over a barbecue for 5–6 minutes, turning them frequently until they are nicely browned all over.

**6** Alternatively, cook the skewers under a conventional grill (broiler). Serve immediately, while still hot.

**Per portion** Energy 256Kcal/1066kJ; Protein 18g; Carbohydrate 12g, of which sugars 4.8g; Fat 15.7g, of which saturates 5.7g; Cholesterol 239mg; Calcium 85mg; Fibre 0.2g; Sodium 192mg

# CRAB AND ASPARAGUS SOUP WITH NUOC CHAM

*In this delicious soup, the recipe has clearly been adapted from the classic French asparagus velouté to produce a much meatier version that has more texture, and the Vietnamese stamp of nuoc cham and nuoc mam.*

**2** Bring to the boil, boil for a few minutes, skim off any foam, then reduce the heat and simmer with the lid on for 1½–2 hours. Remove the lid and simmer for a further 30 minutes to reduce the stock. Skim off any fat, season, then strain the stock and measure out 1.5 litres/2½ pints/6¼ cups.

**3** Heat the oil in a deep pan or wok. Stir in the shallots and garlic, until they begin to colour. Remove from the heat, stir in the flour, and then pour in the stock. Put the pan back over the heat and bring to the boil, stirring constantly, until smooth.

**4** Add the crab meat and asparagus, reduce the heat and leave to simmer for 15–20 minutes. Season to taste with salt and pepper, then ladle the soup into bowls, garnish with fresh basil and coriander leaves, and serve with a splash of *nuoc cham*.

**COOK'S TIP**
If you have a good supply of fresh crabs, increase the quantity of crab meat to make a soup that is rich and filling.

SERVES FOUR

INGREDIENTS
15ml/1 tbsp vegetable oil
2 shallots, finely chopped
2 garlic cloves, finely chopped
15ml/1 tbsp rice flour or cornflour (cornstarch)
225g/8oz/1⅓ cups cooked crab meat, chopped into small pieces
450g/1lb preserved asparagus, finely chopped, or 450g/1lb fresh asparagus, trimmed and steamed
salt and ground black pepper
basil and coriander (cilantro) leaves, to garnish
*nuoc cham*, to serve

For the stock
1 meaty chicken carcass
25g/1oz dried shrimp, soaked in water for 30 minutes, rinsed and drained
2 onions, peeled and quartered
2 garlic cloves, crushed
15ml/1 tbsp *nuoc mam*
6 black peppercorns
sea salt

**1** To make the chicken stock, put the chicken carcass into a large pan. Add all the other stock ingredients, apart from the salt, and then pour in 2 litres/3½ pints/8 cups water. Bring the stock to the boil and boil for a few minutes.

# TOFU SOUP WITH MUSHROOMS AND GINGER

*THIS IS A TYPICAL CANH — A CLEAR BROTH FROM THE NORTH OF VIETNAM. IT SHOULD BE LIGHT, TO BALANCE A MEAL THAT MAY INCLUDE SOME HEAVIER MEAT OR POULTRY DISHES. AS THE SOUP IS RELIANT ON A WELL-FLAVOURED, AROMATIC BROTH, THE BASIC STOCK NEEDS TO BE RICH IN TASTE.*

SERVES FOUR

INGREDIENTS

115g/4oz/scant 2 cups dried shiitake mushrooms, soaked in water for 20 minutes
15ml/1 tbsp vegetable oil
2 shallots, halved and sliced
2 Thai chillies, seeded and sliced
4cm/1½in fresh root ginger, peeled and grated or finely chopped
15ml/1 tbsp *nuoc mam*
350g/12oz tofu, rinsed, drained and cut into bitesize cubes
4 tomatoes, skinned, seeded and cut into thin strips
salt and ground black pepper
1 bunch coriander (cilantro), stalks removed, finely chopped, to garnish

For the stock

1 meaty chicken carcass or 500g/1¼lb pork ribs
25g/1oz dried squid or shrimp, soaked in water for 15 minutes
2 onions, peeled and quartered
2 garlic cloves, crushed
7.5cm/3in fresh root ginger, chopped
15ml/1 tbsp *nuoc mam*
6 black peppercorns
2 star anise
4 cloves
1 cinnamon stick
sea salt

**1** To make the stock, put the chicken carcass or pork ribs in a deep pan. Then drain and rinse the dried squid or shrimp. Add to the pan with the remaining stock ingredients, except the salt, and then pour in 2 litres/3½ pints/8 cups water.

**2** Bring to the boil, and boil for a few minutes, skim off any foam, then reduce the heat and simmer with the lid on for 1½–2 hours. Remove the lid and continue simmering for a further 30 minutes to reduce. Skim off any fat, season, then strain and measure out 1.5 litres/2½ pints/6¼ cups.

**3** Squeeze dry the soaked shiitake mushrooms, remove the stems and slice the caps into thin strips. Heat the oil in a large pan or wok and stir in the shallots, chillies and ginger. As the fragrance begins to rise, stir in the *nuoc mam*, followed by the stock.

**4** Add the tofu, mushrooms and tomatoes and bring the mixture to the boil. Then reduce the heat and simmer the pan or wok for 5–10 minutes. Season to taste and scatter the finely chopped fresh coriander over the top. Serve piping hot.

**Per portion** Energy 220Kcal/919kJ; Protein 12g; Carbohydrate 26g, of which sugars 4g; Fat 8g, of which saturates 1g; Cholesterol 0mg; Calcium 47.8mg; Fibre 1.1g; Sodium 500mg

# BROTH WITH STUFFED CABBAGE LEAVES

*THE ORIGINS OF THIS SOUP, CALLED CANH BAP CUON, COULD BE ATTRIBUTED TO THE FRENCH DISH CHOU FARCI, OR TO THE ANCIENT CHINESE TRADITION OF COOKING DUMPLINGS IN A CLEAR BROTH. THIS VIETNAMESE SOUP IS OFTEN RESERVED FOR SPECIAL OCCASIONS SUCH AS THE NEW YEAR, TET.*

SERVES FOUR

INGREDIENTS
    10 Chinese leaves (Chinese cabbage)
      or Savoy cabbage leaves, halved,
      main ribs removed
    4 spring onions (scallions),
      green tops left whole, white
      part finely chopped
    5–6 dried cloud ear (wood ear)
      mushrooms, soaked in hot water
      for 15 minutes
    115g/4oz minced (ground) pork
    115g/4oz prawns (shrimp), shelled,
      deveined and finely chopped
    1 Thai chilli, seeded and chopped
    30ml/2 tbsp *nuoc mam*
    15ml/1 tbsp soy sauce
    4cm/1½in fresh root ginger, peeled
      and very finely sliced
    chopped fresh coriander (cilantro),
      to garnish
For the stock
    1 meaty chicken carcass
    2 onions, peeled and quartered
    4 garlic cloves, crushed
    4cm/1½in fresh root ginger,
      chopped
    30ml/2 tbsp *nuoc mam*
    30ml/2 tbsp soy sauce
    6 black peppercorns
    a few sprigs of fresh thyme
    sea salt

**1** To make the chicken stock, put the chicken carcass into a deep pan. Add all the other stock ingredients except the sea salt and pour over 2 litres/3½ pints/8 cups of water. Bring to the boil, and boil for a few minutes, skim off any foam, then reduce the heat and simmer gently with the lid on for 1½–2 hours.

**2** Remove the lid and simmer for a further 30 minutes to reduce the stock. Skim off any fat, season with sea salt, then strain the stock and measure out 1.5 litres/2½ pints/6¼ cups. It is important to skim off any froth or fat, so that the broth is light and fragrant.

**3** Blanch the cabbage leaves in boiling water for about 2 minutes, or until tender. Remove with a slotted spoon and refresh under cold water. Add the green tops of the spring onions to the boiling water and blanch for a minute, or until tender, then drain and refresh under cold water. Carefully tear each piece into five thin strips and set aside.

**4** Squeeze dry the cloud ear mushrooms, then trim and finely chop and mix with the pork, prawns, spring onion whites, chilli, *nuoc mam* and soy sauce. Lay a cabbage leaf flat on a surface and place a teaspoon of the filling about 1cm/½in from the bottom edge – the edge nearest to you.

**5** Fold this bottom edge over the filling, and then fold in the sides of the leaf to seal it. Roll all the way to the top of the leaf to form a tight bundle. Wrap a piece of blanched spring onion green around the bundle and tie it so that it holds together. Repeat with the remaining leaves and filling.

**6** Bring the stock to the boil in a wok or deep pan. Stir in the finely sliced ginger, then reduce the heat and drop in the cabbage bundles. Bubble very gently over a low heat for about 20 minutes to ensure that the filling is thoroughly cooked. Serve immediately, ladled into bowls with a sprinkling of fresh coriander leaves.

Per portion Energy 106Kcal/447kJ; Protein 14g; Carbohydrate 9g, of which sugars 1g; Fat 2g, of which saturates 0g; Cholesterol 77mg; Calcium 43mg; Fibre 0.3g; Sodium 1100mg

# SIZZLING SPICED CRÊPES

*FRENCH IN STYLE, BUT VIETNAMESE IN FLAVOUR, THESE DELIGHTFULLY CRISPY, TASTY CRÊPES, MADE WITH COCONUT MILK AND FILLED WITH PRAWNS, MUSHROOMS AND BEANSPROUTS, ARE OUT OF THIS WORLD. YOU CAN MAKE EIGHT SMALL CRÊPES, RATHER THAN FOUR SMALL ONES, IF YOU PREFER.*

SERVES FOUR

INGREDIENTS
115g/4oz/½ cup minced
  (ground) pork
15ml/1 tbsp *nuoc mam*
2 garlic cloves, crushed
175g/6oz/⅔ cup button (white)
  mushrooms, finely sliced
about 60ml/4 tbsp vegetable oil
1 onion, finely sliced
1–2 green or red Thai chillies,
  seeded and finely sliced
115g/4oz prawns (shrimp), shelled
  and deveined
225g/8oz/1 cup beansprouts
1 small bunch fresh coriander
  (cilantro), stalks removed, leaves
  roughly chopped
salt and ground black pepper
*nuoc cham*, to serve
For the batter
115g/4oz/1 cup rice flour
10ml/2 tsp ground turmeric
10ml/2 tsp curry powder
5ml/1 tsp sugar
2.5ml/½ tsp salt
300ml/½ pint/1¼ cups canned
  coconut milk
4 spring onions (scallions), trimmed
  and finely sliced

**1** To make the batter, beat the rice flour, spices, sugar and salt with the coconut milk and 300ml/½ pint/1¼ cups water, until smooth and creamy. Stir in the spring onions and then leave to stand for 30 minutes.

**2** In a bowl, mix the pork with the *nuoc mam*, garlic and seasoning and knead well. Lightly sauté the sliced mushrooms in 15ml/1 tbsp of the oil and set aside.

**3** Heat 10ml/2 tsp of the oil in a non-stick pan. Stir in a quarter of the onion and the chillies, then add a quarter each of the pork and the prawns. Pour in 150ml/¼ pint/⅔ cup of the batter, swirling the pan so that it spreads over the pork and prawns right to the edges.

**4** Pile a quarter of the beansprouts and mushrooms on one side of the crêpe, just in from the middle. Reduce the heat and cover the pan for 2–3 minutes, or until the edges pull away from the sides. Remove the lid and cook the crêpe for another 2 minutes; gently lift up an edge of the crêpe with a spatula to see if it's brown underneath.

**5** Once it is nicely browned, scatter some chopped coriander over the empty side of the crêpe and fold it over the beansprouts and mushrooms. Slide the crêpe on to a plate and keep warm while you make the remaining crêpes in the same way. Serve with *nuoc cham* for dipping, or drizzle with chilli sauce and serve fresh red or green chillies on the side.

Per portion Energy 379Kcal/1581kJ; Protein 18g; Carbohydrate 37g, of which sugars 9g; Fat 18g, of which saturates 3g; Cholesterol 77mg; Calcium 119mg; Fibre 3.2g; Sodium 50mg

# PORK PÂTÉ <u>IN A</u> BANANA LEAF

*THIS PÂTÉ, CHA LUA, HAS A VIETNAMESE TWIST: IT IS STEAMED IN BANANA LEAVES AND HAS A SLIGHTLY SPRINGY TEXTURE AND DELICATE FLAVOUR. BAGUETTES ARE A COMMON SIGHT ALONGSIDE THE NOODLES AND VEGETABLES IN SOUTHERN MARKETS AND FREQUENTLY EATEN SMEARED WITH PÂTÉ.*

SERVES SIX

INGREDIENTS

  45ml/3 tbsp *nuoc mam*
  30ml/2 tbsp vegetable or sesame oil
  15ml/1 tbsp sugar
  10ml/2 tsp five-spice powder
  2 shallots, peeled and finely chopped
  2 garlic cloves, crushed
  750g/1lb 10oz/3¼ cups minced
   (ground) pork
  25g/1oz/¼ cup potato starch
  7.5ml/1½ tsp baking powder
  1 banana leaf, trimmed into a strip
   25cm/10in wide
  vegetable oil, for brushing
  salt and ground black pepper
  *nuoc cham* and a baguette or salad,
   to serve

**1** In a bowl, beat the *nuoc mam* and oil with the sugar and five-spice powder. Once the sugar has dissolved, stir in the shallots and garlic. Add the minced pork and seasoning, and knead well until thoroughly combined. Cover and chill for 2–3 hours.

**2** Knead the mixture again, thumping it down into the bowl to remove any air. Add the potato starch and baking powder and knead until smooth and pasty. Mould the pork mixture into a fat sausage, about 18cm/7in long, and place it on an oiled dish.

**VARIATION**
This pâté can be added to soups and stir-fried dishes, or fried with eggs.

**3** Lay the banana leaf on a flat surface, brush with a little vegetable oil, and place the pork sausage across it. Lift up the edge of the banana leaf nearest to you and fold it over the sausage mixture, tuck in the sides, and roll it up into a firm, tight bundle. Secure with a piece of string, so that it doesn't unravel during the cooking process.

**4** Fill a wok one-third full with water. Balance a bamboo steamer, with its lid on, above the level of the water. Bring to the boil, lift the lid and place the banana leaf bundle on the rack, being careful not to burn yourself. Re-cover and steam for 45 minutes. Leave the pâté to cool in the leaf, open it up and cut it into slices. Drizzle with *nuoc cham*, and serve with a baguette or salad.

**COOK'S TIP**
To prepare banana leaves, trim the leaves to fit the steamer, using a pair of scissors, making sure that there is enough to fold over the pâté. If you cannot find banana leaves, you can use large spring green (collard) leaves, or several Savoy cabbage leaves instead.

**Per portion** Energy 234Kcal/978kJ; Protein 28g; Carbohydrate 8g, of which sugars 3g; Fat 10g, of which saturates 2g; Cholesterol 79mg; Calcium 46mg; Fibre 0.4g; Sodium 700mg

# BACON-WRAPPED BEEF ON SKEWERS

*IN NORTHERN VIETNAM, BEEF OFTEN FEATURES ON THE STREET MENU. GRILLED, STIR-FRIED, OR SITTING MAJESTICALLY IN A STEAMING BOWL OF PHO, BEEF IS USED WITH PRIDE. IN SOUTHERN VIETNAM, SNACKS LIKE THIS ONE WOULD NORMALLY BE MADE WITH PORK OR CHICKEN.*

### SERVES FOUR

INGREDIENTS
   225g/8oz beef fillet or rump, cut
     across the grain into 12 strips
   12 thin strips of streaky (fatty) bacon
   ground black pepper
   4 bamboo skewers, soaked in water
   *nuoc cham*, for dipping
For the marinade
   15ml/1 tbsp groundnut (peanut) oil
   30ml/2 tbsp *nuoc mam*
   30ml/2 tbsp soy sauce
   4–6 garlic cloves, crushed
   10ml/2 tsp sugar

**1** To make the marinade, mix all the marinade ingredients in a large bowl until the sugar dissolves. Season generously with black pepper. Add the beef strips, coating them in the marinade, and set aside for about an hour.

**2** Preheat a griddle pan over a high heat. Roll up each strip of beef and wrap it in a slice of bacon. Thread the rolls on to the skewers, so that you have three on each one.

**3** Cook the bacon-wrapped rolls for 4–5 minutes, turning once, until the bacon is golden and crispy. Serve immediately, with a bowl of *nuoc cham* for dipping.

**Per portion** Energy 279Kcal/1155kJ; Protein 21.7g; Carbohydrate 1.0g, of which sugars 1.0g; Fat 21.3g, of which saturates 7.1g; Cholesterol 69mg; Calcium 6mg; Fibre 0g; Sodium 750mg

# BEEF NOODLE SOUP

*Some would say that this classic noodle soup, pho, is Vietnam in a bowl. Made with beef (pho bo) or chicken (pho ga), it is Vietnamese fast food, street food, working men's food and family food. It is nutritious and filling, and makes an intensely satisfying meal.*

SERVES SIX

INGREDIENTS
  250g/9oz beef sirloin
  500g/1¼lb dried noodles, soaked in
    lukewarm water for 20 minutes
  1 onion, halved and finely sliced
  6–8 spring onions (scallions),
    cut into long pieces
  2–3 red Thai chillies, seeded and
    finely sliced
  115g/4oz/½ cup beansprouts
  1 large bunch each fresh coriander
    (cilantro) and mint, stalks removed,
    leaves chopped
  2 limes, cut in wedges, and hoisin
    sauce, *nuoc mam* or *nuoc cham*
    to serve
For the stock
  1.5kg/3lb 5oz oxtail, trimmed of fat
    and cut into thick pieces
  1kg/2¼lb beef shank or brisket
  2 large onions, peeled and quartered
  2 carrots, peeled and cut into chunks
  7.5cm/3in fresh root ginger,
    cut into chunks
  6 cloves
  2 cinnamon sticks
  6 star anise
  5ml/1 tsp black peppercorns
  30ml/2 tbsp soy sauce
  45–60ml/3–4 tbsp *nuoc mam*
  salt

**1** To make the stock, put the oxtail into a large, deep pan and cover it with water. Bring it to the boil and blanch the meat for about 10 minutes. Drain the meat, rinsing off any scum, and clean out the pan. Put the blanched oxtail back into the pan with the other stock ingredients, apart from the *nuoc mam* and salt, and cover with about 3 litres/5¼ pints/12 cups water. Bring it to the boil, reduce the heat and simmer, covered, for 2–3 hours.

**2** Remove the lid and simmer for another hour, until the stock has reduced to about 2 litres/3½ pints/ 8 cups. Skim off any fat and then strain the stock into another pan.

**3** Cut the beef sirloin across the grain into thin pieces, the size of the heel of your hand. Bring the stock to the boil once more, stir in the *nuoc mam*, season to taste, then reduce the heat and leave the stock simmering until ready to use.

**4** Meanwhile, bring a pan filled with water to the boil, drain the rice sticks and add to the water. Cook for about 5 minutes or until tender – you may need to separate them with a pair of chopsticks if they look as though they are sticking together.

**5** Drain the noodles and divide them equally among six wide soup bowls. Top each serving with the slices of beef, onion, spring onions, chillies and beansprouts.

**6** Ladle the hot stock over the top of these ingredients, top with the fresh herbs and serve with the lime wedges to squeeze over. Pass around the hoisin sauce, *nuoc mam* or *nuoc cham* for those who like a little sweetening, fish flavouring or extra fire.

**COOK'S TIPS**
• The key to *pho* is a tasty, light stock flavoured with ginger, cinnamon, cloves and star anise, so it is worth cooking it slowly and leaving it to stand overnight to allow the flavours to develop fully.
• To enjoy this dish, use your chopsticks to lift the noodles through the layers of flavouring and slurp them up. This is the essence of Vietnam.

**Per portion** Energy 391Kcal/1635kJ; Protein 16g; Carbohydrate 74g, of which sugars 3g; Fat 2g, of which saturates 1g; Cholesterol 21mg; Calcium 62mg; Fibre 0.8g; Sodium 600mg

# SINGAPORE NOODLES

*THE VIETNAMESE HAVE PUT THEIR OWN PARTICULARLY DELICIOUS STAMP ON SINGAPORE NOODLES, WHICH ARE POPULAR THROUGHOUT SOUTH-EAST ASIA. IN HO CHI MINH CITY, THE NOODLES ARE STANDARD STREET AND CAFÉ FOOD, AN IDEAL SNACK FOR ANYONE FEELING A LITTLE PECKISH.*

### SERVES FOUR

INGREDIENTS
    30ml/2 tbsp sesame oil
    1 onion, finely chopped
    3 garlic cloves, finely chopped
    3–4 green or red Thai chillies,
      seeded and finely chopped
    4cm/1½in fresh root ginger,
      peeled and finely chopped
    6 spring onions (scallions),
      finely chopped
    1 skinless chicken breast fillet,
      cut into bitesize strips
    90g/3½oz pork, cut into bitesize
      strips
    90g/3½oz prawns (shrimp), shelled
    2 tomatoes, skinned, seeded
      and chopped
    30ml/2 tbsp tamarind paste
    15ml/1 tbsp *nuoc mam*
    grated rind and juice of 1 lime
    10ml/2 tsp sugar
    150ml/¼ pint/⅔ cup water or
      fish stock
    225g/8oz fresh rice sticks
      (vermicelli)
    salt and ground black pepper
    1 bunch each fresh basil and mint,
      stalks removed, and *nuoc cham*,
      to serve

**1** Heat a wok or heavy pan and add the oil. Stir in the onion, garlic, chillies and ginger, and cook until they begin to colour. Add the spring onions and cook for 1 minute, add the chicken and pork, and cook for 1–2 minutes, then stir in the prawns.

**2** Add the tomatoes, followed by the tamarind paste, *nuoc mam*, lime rind and juice, and sugar. Pour in the water or fish stock, and cook gently for 2–3 minutes. Bubble up the liquid to reduce it.

**VARIATIONS**
• At the Singapore noodle stalls, batches of cold, cooked noodles are kept ready to add to the delicious concoction cooking in the wok. At home, you can make this dish with any kind of noodles – egg or rice, fresh or dried.
• Cured Chinese sausage and snails, or strips of squid, are sometimes added to the mixture to ring the changes.

**3** Meanwhile, toss the noodles in a large pan of boiling water and cook for a few minutes until tender.

**4** Drain the noodles and add to the chicken and prawn mixture. Season with salt and ground black pepper.

**5** Serve immediately, with basil and mint leaves scattered over the top, and drizzled with spoonfuls of *nuoc cham*.

**COOK'S TIP**
It's important to serve this dish immediately once the noodles have been added, otherwise they will go soft.

**Per portion** Energy 420Kcal/1756kJ; Protein 23g; Carbohydrate 59g, of which sugars 9g; Fat 10g, of which saturates 2g; Cholesterol 86mg; Calcium 119mg; Fibre 1.3g; Sodium 500mg

# FISH & SHELLFISH

With its long coastline along the South China Sea and its many rivers including the Red River in the north and the mighty Mekong in the south, Vietnam enjoys an abundance of varied saltwater and freshwater fish and shellfish. These ingredients can be marinated, or cooked, in coconut milk, with liberal quantities of ginger, garlic and chillies, as well as aromatic herbs. This selection includes Braised Eel with Butternut Squash and Lobster and Crab Steamed in Beer.

# HANOI FRIED FISH WITH DILL

*THE NORTH OF VIETNAM IS WELL KNOWN FOR ITS USE OF PUNGENT HERBS, SO MUCH SO THAT A DISH OF NOODLES CAN BE SERVED PLAIN, DRESSED ONLY WITH CORIANDER AND BASIL. IN THIS POPULAR DISH FROM HANOI,* CHA CA HANOI, *THE DILL COMPLEMENTS THE FISH BEAUTIFULLY.*

SERVES FOUR

INGREDIENTS

75g/3oz/⅔ cup rice flour
7.5ml/1½ tsp ground turmeric
500g/1¼lb white fish fillets, such as
   cod, skinned and cut into chunks
vegetable oil, for deep-frying
1 large bunch fresh dill
15ml/1 tbsp groundnut (peanut) oil
30ml/2 tbsp roasted peanuts
4 spring onions (scallions), cut into
   bitesize pieces
1 small bunch fresh basil,
   stalks removed, leaves chopped
1 small bunch fresh coriander
   (cilantro), stalks removed
cooked rice, 1 lime, cut into wedges,
   and *nuoc cham*, to serve

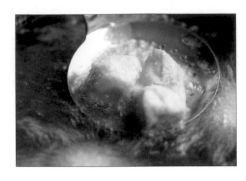

**1** Mix the flour with the ground turmeric and toss the chunks of fish in it until they are well coated. Heat the oil in a wok or a large heavy pan and cook the fish in batches until crisp and golden. Use a perforated ladle to remove the fish from the oil, and drain on kitchen paper.

**2** Scatter some of the dill fronds on a serving dish, arrange the fish on top and keep warm. Chop some of the remaining dill fronds and set aside for the garnish.

**3** Heat the groundnut oil in a small wok or frying pan. Stir in the peanuts and cook for 1 minute, then add the spring onions, the remaining dill fronds, basil and coriander. Stir-fry for no more than 30 seconds, then spoon the herbs and peanuts over the fish. Garnish with the chopped dill and serve with lime wedges and *nuoc cham* to drizzle over the top.

**Per portion** Energy 350Kcal/1458kJ; Protein 27g; Carbohydrate 17g, of which sugars 1g; Fat 19g, of which saturates 3g; Cholesterol 85mg; Calcium 112mg; Fibre 1.2g; Sodium 200mg

# BRAISED EEL <u>WITH</u> BUTTERNUT SQUASH

*ALTHOUGH THIS DISH IS FOUND IN MANY PARTS OF VIETNAM, IT IS TRADITIONALLY A NORTHERN DISH AND IT IS THERE, IN THE HIGHLANDS, THAT IT IS BEST SAMPLED. THE EELS ARE CAUGHT IN THE RED, BLACK AND SONG MA RIVERS, AND THE LOCAL NAME OF THE DISH IS "THREE RIVERS EEL".*

SERVES FOUR

INGREDIENTS
  45ml/3 tbsp raw cane sugar
  30ml/2 tbsp soy sauce
  45ml/3 tbsp *nuoc mam*
  2 garlic cloves, crushed
  2 dried chillies
  2–3 star anise
  4–5 black peppercorns
  350g/12oz eel on the bone, skinned,
    cut into 2.5cm/1in-thick chunks
  200g/7oz butternut squash, cut into
    bitesize chunks
  4 spring onions (scallions), cut into
    bitesize pieces
  30ml/2 tbsp sesame or vegetable oil
  5cm/2in fresh root ginger, peeled
    and cut into matchsticks
  salt
  cooked rice or noodles,
    to serve

**1** Put the raw cane sugar in a wok or heavy pan with 30ml/2 tbsp water, and gently heat it until it turns golden brown. Then remove the pan from the heat and stir in the soy sauce and the *nuoc mam* with 120ml/4fl oz/½ cup water. Add the garlic, chillies, star anise and peppercorns and return the pan to the heat.

**COOK'S TIP**
If you can't find eel, use mackerel for this dish. The fat rendered from these fish melts into the caramel sauce, making it deliciously velvety. It is often served with chopped fresh coriander (cilantro) on top.

**2** Add the eel chunks, squash and spring onions, making sure the fish is well coated in the sauce, and season with salt. Reduce the heat, cover the pan and simmer gently for about 20 minutes, until the eel and vegetables are tender.

**3** Meanwhile, heat a small wok, pour in the oil and stir-fry the ginger until crisp and golden. Remove and drain on kitchen paper.

**4** Serve with rice or noodles, with the crispy ginger sprinkled on top.

**Per portion** Energy 204Kcal/857kJ; Protein 11g; Carbohydrate 20g, of which sugars 14g; Fat 10g, of which saturates 1g; Cholesterol 0mg; Calcium 76mg; Fibre 1g; Sodium 110mg

# MEAT, POULTRY, FROGS & SNAILS

*Chickens and ducks are commonly reared in Vietnam and are sold live in the markets, so that they are fresh for the pot. Pork is the country's principal meat, with every bit put to good use. Beef is common in the north of the country, but more sparingly used in other regions. Containers of hopping frogs are also a familiar sight in local markets. These creatures might be spit-roasted, grilled, stir-fried and stewed, and can be richly spiced, shown here in the recipe for Curried Frog's Legs.*

# BEEF STEW <u>WITH</u> STAR ANISE <u>AND</u> BASIL

*THE VIETNAMESE PRIZE THIS DISH FOR BREAKFAST, AND ON CHILLY MORNINGS PEOPLE QUEUE UP FOR A BOWL OF THIT BO KHO ON THEIR WAY TO WORK. TRADITIONALLY, IT HAS AN ORANGE HUE FROM THE OIL IN WHICH ANNATTO SEEDS HAVE BEEN FRIED, BUT HERE THE COLOUR COMES FROM TURMERIC.*

SERVES FOUR TO SIX

INGREDIENTS

500g/1¼ lb lean beef, cut into
   bitesize cubes
15ml/1 tbsp ground turmeric
30ml/2 tbsp sesame or
   vegetable oil
3 shallots, chopped
3 garlic cloves, chopped
2 red chillies, seeded and chopped
2 lemon grass stalks, cut into several
   pieces and bruised
15ml/1 tbsp curry powder
4 star anise, roasted and ground to
   a powder
700ml/scant 1¼ pints hot beef or
   chicken stock, or boiling water
45ml/3 tbsp *nuoc mam*
30ml/2 tbsp soy sauce
15ml/1 tbsp raw cane sugar
1 bunch fresh basil, stalks removed
salt and ground black pepper
1 onion, halved and finely sliced, and
   chopped fresh coriander (cilantro)
   leaves, to garnish
steamed fragrant or sticky rice, or
   chunks of baguette, to serve

**1** Toss the beef in the ground turmeric and set aside. Heat a wok or heavy pan and add the oil. Stir in the shallots, garlic, chillies and lemon grass, and cook until they become fragrant.

**COOK'S TIP**
If you prefer to use annatto seeds instead of turmeric, they can be found in some Asian supermarkets. Fry 15ml/1 tbsp seeds in a little oil.

**2** Add the curry powder, all but 10ml/2 tsp of the roasted star anise, and the beef. Brown the beef, then pour in the stock or water, *nuoc mam*, soy sauce and sugar. Stir and bring to the boil. Reduce the heat and cook gently for about 40 minutes, or until the meat is tender and the liquid has reduced.

**3** Season to taste with salt and pepper, stir in the reserved roasted star anise, and add the basil. Transfer the stew to a serving dish and garnish with the sliced onion and coriander leaves.

**4** Serve with steamed fragrant or sticky rice, or chunks of baguette.

**Per portion** Energy 314Kcal/1312kJ; Protein 33g; Carbohydrate 17g, of which sugars 11g; Fat 14g, of which saturates 4g; Cholesterol 64mg; Calcium 64mg; Fibre 1.7g; Sodium 150mg

# BEEF SATÉ

*THE SPICY PEANUT PASTE, SATÉ, IS A GREAT FAVOURITE IN SOUTH-EAST ASIA. IT IS THOUGHT TO
HAVE ORIGINATED IN INDIA. IN SOUTHERN VIETNAM, IT IS USED FOR GRILLING AND STIR-FRYING
MEATS AND SEAFOOD, AS WELL AS FOR DRESSING EGG NOODLES AND SPIKING MARINADES.*

SERVES FOUR TO SIX

INGREDIENTS
    500g/1¼lb beef sirloin, cut in
        bitesize pieces
    15ml/1 tbsp groundnut (peanut) oil
    1 bunch rocket (arugula) leaves
For the saté
    60ml/4 tbsp groundnut (peanut) or
        vegetable oil
    5 garlic cloves, crushed
    5 dried Serrano chillies, seeded and
        ground
    10ml/2 tsp curry powder
    50g/2oz/⅓ cup roasted peanuts,
        finely ground

**1** To make the saté, heat the oil in a
wok or heavy pan and stir in the garlic
until it begins to colour. Add the chillies,
curry powder and peanuts and stir over
a gentle heat until the mixture forms a
paste. Remove from the heat and leave
to cool.

**2** Put the beef into a large bowl. Beat
the groundnut oil into the saté and
add the mixture to the pieces of beef.
Mix well, so that the beef is evenly
coated, and put aside to marinate
for 30–40 minutes.

**3** Soak four to six wooden skewers in
water for 30 minutes. Prepare a
barbecue. Thread the meat on to the
skewers and cook for 2–3 minutes on
each side. Serve the meat with the
rocket leaves for wrapping.

**Per portion** Energy 433Kcal/1798kJ; Protein 34g; Carbohydrate 4g, of which sugars 1g; Fat 31g, of which saturates 7g; Cholesterol 64mg; Calcium 68mg; Fibre 1.5g; Sodium 100mg

# VIETNAMESE BEEF FONDUE WITH PINEAPPLE AND ANCHOVY DIPPING SAUCE

*INTRODUCED BY MONGOLIAN TRIBESMEN, AND ADOPTED BY THE CHINESE, BO NHUNG DAM IS AN ANCIENT WAY OF COOKING MEAT. TRADITIONALLY, IT WAS MADE AND SERVED IN A CHINESE LAU, A TURBAN-SHAPED PAN WITH A STOVE UNDERNEATH TO KEEP THE LIQUID SIMMERING.*

SERVES FOUR TO SIX

INGREDIENTS
    30ml/2 tbsp sesame oil
    1 garlic clove, crushed
    2 shallots, finely chopped
    2.5cm/1in fresh root ginger, peeled
       and finely sliced
    1 lemon grass stalk, cut into
       several pieces and bruised
    30ml/2 tbsp sugar
    225ml/8½fl oz/1 cup white rice
       vinegar
    700g/1lb 10oz beef fillet, thinly
       sliced into rectangular strips
    salt and ground black pepper
    chopped or sliced salad vegetables,
       herbs and rice wrappers,
       to serve
For the beef stock
    450g/1lb meaty beef bones
    15ml/1 tbsp soy sauce
    15ml/1 tbsp *nuoc mam*
    1 onion, peeled and quartered
    2.5cm/1in fresh root ginger, peeled
       and chopped
    3 cloves
    1 star anise
    1 cinnamon stick
For the dipping sauce
    15ml/1 tbsp white rice vinegar
    juice of 1 lime
    5ml/1 tsp sugar
    1 garlic clove, peeled and
       chopped
    2 Thai chillies, seeded and
       chopped
    12 canned anchovy fillets, drained
    2 slices of pineapple, centre removed
       and flesh chopped

**COOK'S TIP**
Traditionally, various meats are used for this dish – pork, chicken, and even shellfish and eel. The diners use the rice wrappers to roll up bundles of salad and meat to dip into the sauce. Once all the meat has been cooked, the fragrant broth is poured into bowls to drink.

**1** To make the stock, put the beef bones into a deep pan with the other ingredients and cover with 900ml/1½ pints/3¾ cups water. Bring to the boil, reduce the heat and simmer, covered, for 1–2 hours. Remove the lid, turn up the heat and gently boil the stock for a further 30–40 minutes, or until it has reduced. Strain and season with salt. Measure out 300ml/½ pint/1¼ cups and set aside.

**2** Meanwhile, make the dipping sauce. In a bowl, mix the vinegar and lime juice with the sugar, until the sugar dissolves. Using a mortar and pestle, crush the garlic and chillies together to form a paste. Add the anchovy fillets and pound them to a paste, then add the pineapple and pound it to a pulp. Stir in the vinegar and lime juice mixture, and set aside.

**VARIATION**
You could use any dipping sauce of your choice, such as sweet and sour peanut sauce.

**3** When ready to eat, heat 15ml/1 tbsp of the sesame oil in a heavy pan, wok or fondue pot. Quickly stir-fry the garlic, shallots, ginger and lemon grass until fragrant and golden, then add the sugar, vinegar, beef stock and the remaining sesame oil. Bring to the boil, stirring constantly until the sugar has dissolved. Season to taste with salt and plenty of freshly ground black pepper.

**4** Transfer the pan or fondue pot to a lighted burner at the table. Lay the beef strips on a large serving dish, and put the dipping sauce in a serving bowl. Using chopsticks or fondue forks, each person cooks their own meat in the broth and dips it into the sauce. Serve with salad vegetables, chopped herbs and rice wrappers.

**Per portion** Energy 412Kcal/1712kJ; Protein 41g; Carbohydrate 17g, of which sugars 15g; Fat 19g, of which saturates 6g; Cholesterol 112mg; Calcium 54mg; Fibre 0.8g; Sodium 1000mg

# BAKED CINNAMON MEAT LOAF

*SIMILAR TO THE VIETNAMESE STEAMED PÂTÉS, THIS TYPE OF MEAT LOAF IS USUALLY SERVED AS A SNACK OR LIGHT LUNCH, WITH A CRUSTY BAGUETTE. ACCOMPANIED WITH EITHER TART PICKLES OR A CRUNCHY SALAD, AND SPLASHED WITH PIQUANT SAUCE, IT IS LIGHT AND TASTY.*

## SERVES FOUR TO SIX

### INGREDIENTS
30ml/2 tbsp *nuoc mam*
25ml/1½ tbsp ground cinnamon
10ml/2 tsp sugar
5ml/1 tsp ground black pepper
15ml/1 tbsp potato starch
450g/1lb lean minced (ground) pork
25g/1oz pork fat, very finely chopped
2–3 shallots, very finely chopped
oil, for greasing
chilli oil or *nuoc cham*, for drizzling
red chilli strips, to garnish
bread or noodles, to serve

**2** Add the minced pork, the chopped pork fat, and the shallots to the bowl and mix thoroughly. Cover and put in the refrigerator for 3–4 hours.

**4** Cover with foil and bake in the oven for 35–40 minutes. If you want the top to turn brown and crunchy, remove the foil for the last 10 minutes.

**1** In a large bowl, mix together the *nuoc mam*, ground cinnamon, sugar and ground black pepper. Beat in the potato starch.

**3** Preheat the oven to 180°C/350°F/ Gas 4. Lightly oil a baking tin (pan) and spread the pork mixture in it – it should feel springy from the potato starch.

**5** Turn the meat loaf out on to a board and slice it into strips. Drizzle the strips with chilli oil or *nuoc cham*, and serve them hot with bread or noodles.

### COOK'S TIPS
• Serve the meat loaf as a nibble with drinks by cutting it into bitesize squares or fingers.
• Serve with a piquant sauce for dipping.
• Cut the meat loaf into wedges and take on a picnic to eat with bread and pickles or chutney.
• Fry slices of meat loaf until browned and serve with fried eggs.

**Per portion** Energy 111Kcal/465kJ; Protein 16g; Carbohydrate 4.8g, of which sugars 2.3g; Fat 3g, of which saturates 1g; Cholesterol 47mg; Calcium 9mg; Fibre 0.2g; Sodium 54mg

# STIR-FRIED PORK RIBS

*ADAPTED FROM THE CLASSIC CHINESE SWEET-AND-SOUR SPARE RIBS, THE VIETNAMESE VERSION INCLUDES BASIL LEAVES AND THE FISH SAUCE, NUOC MAM. THIS IS FINGER FOOD, REQUIRING FINGER BOWLS, AND IS PERFECT SERVED WITH STICKY RICE AND A SALAD.*

SERVES FOUR TO SIX

INGREDIENTS

45ml/3 tbsp hoisin sauce
45ml/3 tbsp *nuoc mam*
10ml/2 tsp five-spice powder
45ml/3 tbsp vegetable or sesame oil
900g/2lb pork ribs
3 garlic cloves, crushed
4cm/1½in fresh root ginger, peeled and grated
1 bunch fresh basil, stalks removed, leaves shredded

**1** In a bowl, mix together the hoisin sauce, *nuoc mam* and five-spice powder with 15ml/1 tbsp of the oil.

**2** Bring a large wok or pan of water to the boil, then add the pork ribs, bring back to the boil and blanch for 10 minutes. Lift the pork ribs out with a slotted spoon and drain thoroughly, then set aside.

**3** Heat the remaining oil in a clean wok. Add the crushed garlic and grated ginger and cook, stirring, until fragrant, then add the blanched pork ribs.

**4** Stir-fry for about 5 minutes, or until the ribs are well browned, then add the hoisin sauce mixture, turning the ribs so that each one is thoroughly coated. Continue stir-frying for 10–15 minutes, or until there is almost no liquid in the wok and the ribs are caramelized and slightly blackened. Add the shredded basil leaves and stir. Serve the ribs straight from the pan, offering dinner guests finger bowls and plenty of napkins to wipe sticky fingers.

**Per portion** Energy 470Kcal/1965kJ; Protein 44g; Carbohydrate 6g, of which sugars 3g; Fat 31g, of which saturates 12g; Cholesterol 149mg; Calcium 98mg; Fibre 0.1g; Sodium 800mg

# VIETNAMESE ROAST DUCK

*THIS DISH, VIT QUAY, IS VIETNAM'S ANSWER TO PEKING DUCK, ALTHOUGH HERE THE SUCCULENT, CRISPY BIRD IS ENJOYED IN ONE COURSE. IN A VIETNAMESE HOME, THE DUCK IS SERVED WITH PICKLED VEGETABLES OR A SALAD, SEVERAL DIPPING SAUCES, AND A FRAGRANT STEAMED RICE.*

SERVES FOUR TO SIX

INGREDIENTS
    1 duck, about 2.25kg/5lb
    90g/3½oz fresh root ginger,
        peeled, roughly chopped and
        lightly crushed
    4 garlic cloves, peeled and crushed
    1 lemon grass stalk, halved and
        bruised
    4 spring onions (scallions), halved
        and crushed
    ginger dipping sauce, *nuoc mam
        gung*, pickled vegetables and
        salad leaves, to serve
For the marinade
    80ml/3fl oz *nuoc mam*
    30ml/2 tbsp soy sauce
    30ml/2 tbsp honey
    15ml/1 tbsp five-spice powder
    5ml/1 tsp ground ginger

**1** In a bowl, beat all the ingredients for the marinade together until they are well blended. Then rub the skin of the duck lightly in order to loosen it, until you can get your fingers between the skin and the meat. Rub the marinade all over the duck, inside its skin and out, then place the duck on a rack over a tray and put it in the refrigerator for 24 hours.

**2** Preheat the oven to 220ºC/425ºF/ Gas 7. Stuff the ginger, garlic, lemon grass and spring onions into the duck's cavity and tie the legs with string. Using a bamboo or metal skewer, poke holes in the skin, including the legs.

**3** Place the duck, breast side down, on a rack over a roasting pan and cook it in the oven for 45 minutes, basting from time to time with the juices that have dripped into the pan. After 45 minutes, turn the duck over so that it is breast side up. Baste it generously and return it to the oven for a further 45 minutes, basting it every 15 minutes. The duck is ready once the juices run clear when the bird is pierced with a skewer.

**4** Serve immediately, pulling at the skin and meat with your fingers, rather than neatly carving it. Serve with ginger dipping sauce, *nuoc mam gung*, pickled vegetables and salad leaves for wrapping up the morsels.

**Per portion** Energy 228Kcal/960kJ; Protein 27g; Carbohydrate 13g, of which sugars 7g; Fat 8g, of which saturates 3g; Cholesterol 131mg; Calcium 69mg; Fibre 0.3g; Sodium 140mg

# VIETNAMESE LEMON GRASS SNAILS

*THE LIVE SNAILS SOLD IN VIETNAMESE MARKETS ARE USUALLY DESTINED FOR THIS POPULAR DELICACY. SERVED STRAIGHT FROM THE BAMBOO STEAMER, THESE LEMON GRASS-INFUSED MORSELS ARE SERVED AS AN APPETIZER, OR AS A SPECIAL SNACK, DIPPED IN NUOC CHAM.*

SERVES FOUR

INGREDIENTS

24 fresh snails in their shells
225g/8oz lean minced (ground) pork,
  passed through the mincer twice
3 lemon grass stalks, trimmed
  and finely chopped or ground
  (reserve the outer leaves)
2 spring onions (scallions),
  finely chopped
25g/1oz fresh root ginger, peeled and
  finely grated
1 red Thai chilli, seeded and
  finely chopped
10ml/2 tsp sesame or groundnut
  (peanut) oil
sea salt and ground black pepper
*nuoc cham* or other sauce,
  for dipping

**1** Pull the snails out of their shells and place them in a colander. Rinse the snails thoroughly in plenty of cold water and pat dry with kitchen paper. Rinse the shells and leave to drain.

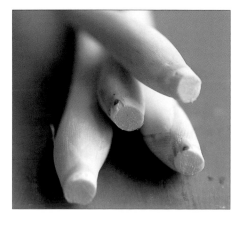

**2** Chop the snails finely and put them in a bowl. Add the minced pork, lemon grass, spring onions, ginger, chilli and oil. Season with salt and pepper and mix all the ingredients together.

**3** Select the best of the lemon grass leaves and tear each one into thin ribbons, roughly 7.5cm/3in long. Bend each ribbon in half and put it inside a snail shell, so that the ends are poking out. The idea is that each diner pulls the ends of the lemon grass ribbon to gently prize the steamed morsel out of its shell.

**COOK'S TIP**
The idea of eating snails may have come from the French, but the method of cooking them in Vietnam is very different. Fresh snails in their shells are available in South-east Asian markets, and in some supermarkets and delicatessens. If you ask for snails in a Vietnamese restaurant, they are likely to be cooked this way.

**4** Using your fingers, stuff each shell with the snail and pork mixture, gently pushing it between the lemon grass ends to the back of the shell so that it fills the shell completely.

**5** Fill a wok or large pan a third of the way up with water and bring it to the boil. Arrange the snail shells, open side up, in a steamer that fits the wok or pan.

**6** Place the lid on the steamer and steam for about 10 minutes, until the mixture is cooked. Serve hot with *nuoc cham* or another strong-flavoured dipping sauce of your choice, such as soy sauce spiked with chopped chillies.

**Per portion** Energy 136Kcal/573kJ; Protein 24.1g; Carbohydrate 0.2g, of which sugars 0.2g; Fat 4.3g, of which saturates 1.1g; Cholesterol 70mg; Calcium 9mg; Fibre 0.1g; Sodium 700mg

# RICE & NOODLES

*Rice or noodles form part of every Vietnamese meal. They are sometimes presented as a main dish, such as Rice with Chicken, Mint and Nuoc Cham, or Noodles with Crab and Cloud Ear Mushrooms, or as standard accompaniments to a meal, such as Steamed Rice and Fresh Rice Noodles. Other rice or noodle dishes, such as Stir-fried Rice with Chinese Sausage, are popular for snacks.*

# STEAMED RICE

*LONG GRAIN RICE IS THE MOST FREQUENTLY EATEN GRAIN IN VIETNAM — FRESHLY STEAMED AND SERVED AT ALMOST EVERY MEAL. IF THE MAIN DISH DOESN'T INCLUDE NOODLES, THEN A BOWL OF STEAMED RICE — COM — OR RICE WRAPPERS WILL PROVIDE THE STARCH FOR THE MEAL.*

SERVES FOUR

INGREDIENTS
  225g/8oz/generous 1 cup long grain
    rice, rinsed and drained
  a pinch of salt

**1** Put the rice into a heavy pan or clay pot. Add 600ml/1 pint/2½ cups water to cover the rice by 2.5cm/1in. Add the salt, and then bring the water to the boil.

**VARIATION**
Jasmine rice is delicious and readily available from Asian stores.

**2** Reduce the heat, cover the pan and cook gently for about 20 minutes, or until all the water has been absorbed. Remove the pan from the heat and leave to steam, still covered, for a further 5–10 minutes.

**3** To serve, simply fluff up with a fork.

**Per portion** Energy 203Kcal/864kJ; Protein 4g; Carbohydrate 49g, of which sugars 0g; Fat 1g, of which saturates 0g; Cholesterol 0mg; Calcium 2mg; Fibre 0.3g; Sodium 0mg

# RICE ROLLS STUFFED WITH PORK

*This traditional Vietnamese dish, Banh cuon, is a classic. The steamed rice sheets are filled with minced pork, rolled up, drizzled in spring onion oil, and then dipped in nuoc cham. Generally, they are eaten as a snack, or served as a starter to a meal.*

SERVES SIX

INGREDIENTS

    25g/1oz dried cloud ear (wood ear)
    mushrooms, soaked in warm water
    for 30 minutes
    350g/12oz minced (ground) pork
    30ml/2 tbsp *nuoc mam*
    10ml/2 tsp sugar
    15ml/1 tbsp vegetable or groundnut
    (peanut) oil
    2 garlic cloves, finely chopped
    2 shallots, finely chopped
    2 spring onions (scallions), trimmed
    and finely chopped
    24 fresh rice sheets, 7.5cm/3in square
    ground black pepper
    spring onion oil, for drizzling
    *nuoc cham*, for dipping

**COOK'S TIP**
To make life easy, prepared, fresh rice sheets are available in Asian markets.

**1** Drain the mushrooms and squeeze out any excess water. Cut off and discard the hard stems. Finely chop the rest of the mushrooms and put them in a bowl. Add the minced pork, *nuoc mam*, and sugar and mix well.

**2** Heat the oil in a wok or heavy pan. Add the garlic, shallots and onions. Stir-fry until golden. Add the pork mixture and stir-fry for 5–6 minutes, until the pork is cooked. Season with pepper.

**3** Place the rice sheets on a flat surface. Spoon a tablespoon of the pork mixture onto the middle of each sheet. Fold one side over the filling, tuck in the sides, and roll to enclose the filling, so that it resembles a short spring roll.

**4** Place the filled rice rolls on a serving plate, drizzle with spring onion oil, and serve with *nuoc cham* or any other chilli or tangy sauce of your choice, for dipping.

**Per portion** Energy 183Kcal/765kJ; Protein 12g; Carbohydrate 16.2g, of which sugars 2.4g; Fat 8g, of which saturates 2g; Cholesterol 39mg; Calcium 11mg; Fibre 0.2g; Sodium 41mg

# STIR-FRIED RICE WITH CHINESE SAUSAGE

*TRADITIONAL VIETNAMESE STIR-FRIED RICE INCLUDES CHINESE PORK SAUSAGE, OR STRIPS OF PORK COMBINED WITH PRAWNS OR CRAB. PREPARED THIS WAY, THE DISH CAN BE EATEN AS A SNACK, OR AS PART OF THE MEAL WITH GRILLED AND ROASTED MEATS ACCOMPANIED BY A VEGETABLE DISH OR SALAD.*

SERVES FOUR

INGREDIENTS
    25g/1oz dried cloud ear (wood ear)
        mushrooms, soaked for 20 minutes
    15ml/1 tbsp vegetable or sesame oil
    1 onion, sliced
    2 green or red Thai chillies, seeded
        and finely chopped
    2 Chinese sausages (15cm/6in long),
        each sliced into 10 pieces
    175g/6oz prawns (shrimp), shelled
        and deveined
    30ml/2 tbsp *nuoc mam*, plus extra
        for drizzling
    10ml/2 tsp five-spice powder
    1 bunch of fresh coriander (cilantro),
        stalks removed, leaves finely
        chopped
    450g/1lb/4 cups cold steamed rice
    ground black pepper

**1** Drain the soaked cloud ear mushrooms and cut them into strips. Heat a wok or heavy pan and add the oil. Add the onion and chillies. Fry until they begin to colour, then stir in the mushrooms.

**COOK'S TIP**
The rice used in these stir-fries is usually made the day before and added cold to the dish.

**2** Add the sausage slices, moving them around the wok or pan until they begin to brown. Add the prawns and move them around until they turn opaque. Stir in the *nuoc mam*, the five-spice powder and 30ml/2 tbsp of the coriander.

**3** Season well with pepper, then quickly add the rice, making sure it doesn't stick to the pan. As soon as the rice is heated through, sprinkle with the remainder of the coriander and serve with *nuoc mam* to drizzle over it.

**Per portion** Energy 398Kcal/1673kJ; Protein 19g; Carbohydrate 44g, of which sugars 4g; Fat 18g, of which saturates 5g; Cholesterol 116mg; Calcium 158mg; Fibre 2g; Sodium 800mg

# RICE CAKES <u>WITH</u> PORK <u>AND</u> LOTUS SEEDS

*IN THE OLD IMPERIAL CITY OF HUE, THIS TRADITIONAL DISH, HUE COM SEN, IS PRESENTED LIKE A
BEAUTIFUL WOMAN, DRESSED IN A LOTUS LEAF AND GARNISHED WITH A FRESH LOTUS FLOWER. SERVE
THE RICE CAKES WITH A SALAD AND DIPPING SAUCE.*

MAKES TWO CAKES

INGREDIENTS
  15ml/1 tbsp vegetable oil
  2 garlic cloves, chopped
  225g/8oz lean pork, cut into
    bitesize chunks
  30ml/2 tbsp *nuoc mam*
  2.5ml/½ tsp sugar
  10ml/2 tsp ground black pepper
  115g/4oz lotus seeds, soaked for
    6 hours and drained
  2 lotus or banana leaves, trimmed
    and cut into 25cm/10in squares
  500g/1¼ lb/5 cups cooked sticky rice
  salt

**1** Heat the oil in a heavy pan. Stir in the
garlic, until it begins to colour, then add
the pork, *nuoc mam*, sugar and pepper.
Cover and cook over a low heat for
about 45 minutes, or until the pork is
tender. Leave to cool.

**2** Meanwhile, bring a pan of salted water
to the boil. Reduce the heat and add the
prepared lotus seeds. Allow them to cook
for 10 minutes, or until they are tender,
then drain, pat dry and leave to cool.

**VARIATIONS**
For celebrations over New Year, Tet, there
is a similar dish called *banh chung,* which
contains mung beans instead of lotus
seeds. In southern Vietnam, banana
leaves are used to make these parcels,
and they make the perfect substitute.
Banana leaves are available in most Asian
markets, and lotus seeds can be found in
Chinese stores.

**3** Using your fingers, shred the cooked
pork and place beside the lotus seeds.
Lay a lotus leaf or banana leaf on a flat
surface and place a quarter of the
cooked sticky rice in the middle of the
leaf. Flatten the centre of the rice
mound slightly and then scatter with
half the shredded pork and half the
lotus seeds.

**4** Drizzle some of the cooking juices
from the pork over the top. Place
another quarter of the rice on top,
moulding and patting it with your
fingers to make sure the pork and lotus
seeds are enclosed like a cake. Fold the
leaf edge nearest to you over the rice,
tuck in the sides, and fold the whole
packet over to form a tight, square
bundle. Tie it with string to secure it
and set aside. Repeat with the second
leaf and the remaining ingredients.

**5** Fill a wok one-third full of water. Place
a double-tiered bamboo steamer, with
its lid on, on top. Bring the water to the
boil, lift the bamboo lid and place a rice
cake on the rack in each tier. Cover and
steam for about 45 minutes. Carefully
open up the parcels and serve.

**Per portion** Energy 736Kcal/3071kJ; Protein 42g; Carbohydrate 52g, of which sugars 2g; Fat 41g, of which saturates 5g; Cholesterol 1mg; Calcium 107mg; Fibre 3.7g; Sodium 700mg

# RICE <u>WITH</u> CHICKEN, MINT <u>AND</u> NUOC CHAM

*FROM THE NORTH OF VIETNAM, THIS REFRESHING DISH CAN BE SERVED SIMPLY, DRIZZLED WITH NUOC CHAM, OR AS PART OF A CELEBRATORY MEAL THAT MIGHT INCLUDE FISH OR CHICKEN, EITHER GRILLED OR ROASTED WHOLE, AND ACCOMPANIED BY PICKLES AND A TABLE SALAD.*

**2** Put the rice in a heavy pan and stir in the stock. When the rice settles, check that the stock sits roughly 2.5cm/1in above the rice; if not, top it up. Bring the liquid to the boil, cover the pan and cook for about 25 minutes, or until all the water has been absorbed.

**3** Remove the pan from the heat and, using a fork, add the shredded chicken, shallots and most of the mint. Cover the pan again and leave the flavours to mingle for 10 minutes. Tip the rice into bowls, or on to a serving dish, garnish with the remaining mint and the spring onions, and serve with *nuoc cham*.

SERVES FOUR

INGREDIENTS
   350g/12oz/1¾ cups long grain rice,
     rinsed and drained
   2–3 shallots, halved and finely sliced
   1 bunch of fresh mint, stalks
     removed, leaves finely shredded
   2 spring onions (scallions), finely
     sliced, to garnish
   *nuoc cham*, to serve
For the stock
   2 meaty chicken legs
   1 onion, peeled and quartered
   4cm/1½in fresh root ginger, peeled
     and coarsely chopped
   15ml/1 tbsp *nuoc mam*
   3 black peppercorns
   1 bunch of fresh mint
   sea salt

**1** To make the stock, put the chicken legs into a deep pan. Add all the other ingredients, except the salt, and pour in 1 litre/1¾ pints/4 cups water. Bring the water to the boil, skim off any foam, then reduce the heat and simmer gently with the lid on for 1 hour. Remove the lid, increase the heat and simmer for a further 30 minutes to reduce the stock. Skim off any fat, strain the stock and season with salt. Measure 750ml/1¼ pints/3 cups stock. Remove the chicken meat from the bone and shred.

**MAKING A MEAL OF IT**
To serve this dish as a meal on its own, stir-fry strips of pork, slices of Chinese sausage and a handful of prawns (shrimp) and toss into the rice along with the shredded chicken.

**Per portion** Energy 370Kcal/1569kJ; Protein 12g; Carbohydrate 79g, of which sugars 1g; Fat 3g, of which saturates 0g; Cholesterol 26mg; Calcium 41mg; Fibre 0.8g; Sodium 200mg

# FRESH RICE NOODLES

*A VARIETY OF DRIED NOODLES IS AVAILABLE IN ASIAN SUPERMARKETS, BUT FRESH ONES ARE QUITE DIFFERENT AND NOT THAT DIFFICULT TO MAKE. THE FRESHLY MADE NOODLE SHEETS CAN BE SERVED AS A SNACK, DRENCHED IN SUGAR OR HONEY, OR DIPPED INTO A SAVOURY SAUCE OF YOUR CHOICE.*

SERVES FOUR

INGREDIENTS
  225g/8oz/2 cups rice flour
  600ml/1 pint/2½ cups water
  a pinch of salt
  15ml/1 tbsp vegetable oil, plus extra
    for brushing
  slivers of red chilli and fresh root
    ginger, and coriander (cilantro)
    leaves, to garnish (optional)

**1** Place the flour in a bowl and stir in some of the water to form a paste. Pour in the rest of the water, beating it to make a lump-free batter. Add the salt and oil and leave to stand for 15 minutes.

**COOK'S TIP**
You may need to top up the water through one of the slits and tighten the cloth.

**2** Meanwhile, fill a wide pan with water. Cut a piece of smooth cotton cloth a little larger than the diameter of the pan. Stretch it over the top of the pan, pulling the edges tautly down over the sides, then wind a piece of string around the edge, to secure. Using a sharp knife, make three small slits, about 2.5cm/1in from the edge of the cloth, at regular intervals.

**3** Bring the water to the boil. Stir the batter and ladle 30–45ml/2–3 tbsp on to the cloth, swirling it to form a 13–15cm/5–6in wide circle. Cover with a domed lid, such as a wok lid, and steam for 1 minute, or until the noodle sheet is translucent.

**4** Carefully insert a spatula or knife under the noodle sheet and prise it off the cloth. (If it doesn't peel off easily, you may need to steam it a little longer.) Transfer the noodle sheet to a lightly oiled baking tray, brush lightly with oil, and cook the remaining batter in the same way.

**VARIATION**
Fresh noodles are also delicious cut into strips and stir-fried with garlic, ginger, chillies and *nuoc cham* or soy sauce.

**Per portion** Energy 251Kcal/1046kJ; Protein 4g; Carbohydrate 45g, of which sugars 0g; Fat 5g, of which saturates 1g; Cholesterol 0mg; Calcium 24mg; Fibre 1.1g; Sodium 200mg

# CRISPY EGG NOODLE PANCAKE WITH PRAWNS, SCALLOPS AND SQUID

*IN DISHES OF CHINESE ORIGIN, EGG NOODLES ARE USED INSTEAD OF RICE NOODLES. FOR THIS POPULAR DISH, THE VIETNAMESE PREFER TO USE THIN SHANGHAI-STYLE NOODLES, WHICH ARE AVAILABLE ONLY IN CHINESE AND ASIAN MARKETS. SERVE WITH A SALAD OR PICKLED VEGETABLES.*

SERVES FOUR

INGREDIENTS

    225g/8oz fresh egg noodles
    60–75ml/4–5 tbsp vegetable oil,
      plus extra for brushing
    4cm/1½in fresh root ginger, peeled
      and cut into matchsticks
    4 spring onions (scallions), trimmed
      and cut into bitesize pieces
    1 carrot, peeled and cut into thin,
      diagonal slices
    8 scallops (halved if large)
    8 baby squid, cut in half
      lengthways
    8 tiger prawns (shrimp), shelled
      and deveined
    30ml/2 tbsp *nuoc mam*
    45ml/3 tbsp soy sauce
    5ml/1 tsp sugar
    ground black pepper
    fresh coriander (cilantro) leaves,
      to garnish
    *nuoc cham* and/or pickled vegetables,
      to serve

**2** Heat 30ml/2 tbsp of the oil in a non-stick, heavy pan. Carefully slide the noodle pancake off the plate into the pan and cook over a medium heat until it is crisp and golden underneath. Add 15ml/1 tbsp oil to the pan, flip the noodle pancake over and crisp the other side too.

**3** Meanwhile, heat a wok or heavy pan and add the remaining oil. Stir in the ginger and spring onions, and cook until they become fragrant. Add the carrot slices, tossing them in the wok, for 1–2 minutes.

**COOK'S TIP**
You can usually ask your fishmonger to prepare the squid, but to prepare squid yourself, get a firm hold of the head and pull it from the body. Reach down inside the body sac and pull out the transparent back bone, as well as any stringy parts. Rinse the body sac inside and out and pat dry. Cut the tentacles off above the eyes and add to the pile of squid you're going to cook. Discard everything else.

**4** Add the scallops, squid and prawns, moving them around the wok, so that they sear while cooking. Stir in the *nuoc mam*, soy sauce and sugar and season well with black pepper.

**5** Transfer the crispy noodle pancake to a serving dish and tip the seafood on top. Garnish with coriander and serve immediately. To eat, break off pieces of the seafood-covered noodle pancake and drizzle with *nuoc cham*.

**1** Bring a large pan of water to the boil. Drop in the noodles, untangling them with chopsticks or a fork. Cook for about 5 minutes, or until tender. Drain thoroughly and spread the noodles out into a wide, thick pancake on a lightly oiled plate. Leave the noodles to dry out a little, so that the pancake holds its shape when it is fried. Noodle nests are a good base for many dishes.

**Per portion** Energy 807Kcal/3401kJ; Protein 83g; Carbohydrate 53g, of which sugars 48g; Fat 31g, of which saturates 5g; Cholesterol 97.5mg; Calcium 110mg; Fibre 2.3g; Sodium 160mg

# NOODLES WITH CRAB AND CLOUD EAR MUSHROOMS

*THIS IS A DISH OF CONTRASTING FLAVOURS, TEXTURES AND COLOURS, AND IN VIETNAM IT IS COOKED WITH SKILL AND DEXTERITY. WHILE ONE HAND GENTLY TURNS THE NOODLES IN THE PAN, THE OTHER TAKES CHUNKS OF FRESH CRAB MEAT AND DROPS THEM INTO THE STEAMING WOK TO SEAL.*

SERVES FOUR

INGREDIENTS

　25g/1oz dried cloud ear (wood ear)
　　mushrooms, soaked in warm water
　　for 20 minutes
　115g/4oz dried bean thread
　　(cellophane) noodles, soaked in
　　warm water for 20 minutes
　30ml/2 tbsp vegetable or sesame oil
　3 shallots, halved and thinly sliced
　2 garlic cloves, crushed
　2 green or red Thai chillies, seeded
　　and sliced
　1 carrot, peeled and cut into thin
　　diagonal rounds
　5ml/1 tsp sugar
　45ml/3 tbsp oyster sauce
　15ml/1 tbsp soy sauce
　400ml/14fl oz/1⅔ cups water or
　　chicken stock
　225g/8oz fresh, raw crab meat, cut
　　into bitesize chunks
　ground black pepper
　fresh coriander (cilantro) leaves,
　　to garnish

**1** Remove the centres from the soaked cloud ear mushrooms and cut the mushrooms in half. Drain the soaked noodles and cut them into 30cm/12in pieces and put aside.

**2** Heat a wok or pan and add 15ml/1 tbsp of the oil. Stir in the shallots, garlic and chillies, and cook until fragrant. Add the carrot rounds and cook for 1 minute, then add the mushrooms. Stir in the sugar with the oyster and soy sauces, followed by the bean thread noodles. Pour in the water or stock, cover the wok or pan and cook for about 5 minutes, or until the noodles are soft and have absorbed most of the sauce.

**3** Meanwhile, heat the remaining oil in a heavy pan. Add the crab meat and cook until it is nicely pink and tender. Season well with black pepper. Arrange the noodles and crab meat on a serving dish and garnish with coriander.

Per portion Energy 292Kcal/1224kJ; Protein 16g; Carbohydrate 30g, of which sugars 5g; Fat 13g, of which saturates 2g; Cholesterol 36mg; Calcium 29mg; Fibre 2.5g; Sodium 1000mg

# FRIED NOODLES <u>WITH</u> SPICY PEANUT SATÉ, BEEF <u>AND</u> FRAGRANT HERBS

*IF YOU LIKE CHILLIES AND PEANUTS, THIS DELICIOUS DISH MAKES THE PERFECT CHOICE. THE STRINGY RICE STICKS ARE FIDDLY TO STIR-FRY AS THEY HAVE A TENDENCY TO CLING TO ONE ANOTHER, SO WORK QUICKLY. THIS DISH IS USUALLY SERVED WITH A TABLE SALAD OR PICKLES.*

## SERVES FOUR

INGREDIENTS

15–30ml/1–2 tbsp vegetable oil
300g/11oz beef sirloin, cut against
    the grain into thin slices
225g/8oz dried rice sticks (vermicelli),
    soaked in warm water for 20 minutes
225g/8oz/1 cup beansprouts
5–10ml/1–2 tsp *nuoc mam*
1 small bunch each of fresh basil
    and mint, stalks removed, leaves
    shredded, to garnish
pickles, to serve

For the saté
4 dried Serrano chillies, seeded
60ml/4 tbsp groundnut (peanut) oil
4–5 garlic cloves, crushed
5–10ml/1–2 tsp curry powder
40g/1½oz/⅓ cup roasted peanuts,
    finely ground

**1** To make the saté, grind the Serrano chillies in a mortar with a pestle. Heat the oil in a heavy pan and stir in the garlic until it begins to colour. Add the chillies, curry powder and the peanuts and stir over a low heat, until the mixture forms a paste. Remove the pan from the heat and leave the mixture to cool.

**2** Heat a wok or heavy pan, and pour in 15ml/1 tbsp of the oil. Add the sliced beef and cook for 1–2 minutes, and stir in 7.5ml/1½ tsp of the spicy peanut saté. Tip the beef on to a clean plate and set aside. Drain the rice sticks.

**VARIATION**
Although it is quite similar to *pad Thai*, one of the national noodle dishes of Thailand, the addition of *nuoc mam*, basil and mint give this fragrant dish a distinctly Vietnamese flavour. There are many similar versions throughout Southeast Asia, made with prawns (shrimp), pork and chicken.

**3** Add 7.5ml/1½ tsp oil to the wok and add the rice sticks and 15ml/1 tbsp saté. Toss the noodles until coated in the sauce and cook for 4–5 minutes, or until tender. Toss in the beef for 1 minute, then add the beansprouts with the *nuoc mam*. Tip the noodles on to a serving dish and sprinkle with the basil and mint. Serve with pickles.

**Per portion** Energy 603Kcal/2507kJ; Protein 26g; Carbohydrate 52g, of which sugars 2g; Fat 32g, of which saturates 6g; Cholesterol 38mg; Calcium 73mg; Fibre 2.2g; Sodium 200mg

# VEGETABLES, SALADS & SAUCES

Raw, stir-fried, braised, pickled or salted, the Vietnamese
include vegetables in every meal. Raw vegetables are enjoyed
pickled or in salads such as Chicken and Shredded Cabbage
Salad, and many dishes are served with a raw vegetable
accompaniment that includes lettuce leaves to wrap around the
food. The Vietnamese love to dip their food, and dips, sauces
and condiments include the popular chilli dipping sauce, Nuoc
Cham, and the hot peanut dipping sauce, Nuoc Leo.

# DEEP-FRIED VEGETABLES WITH NUOC CHAM

*STIR-FRIED, STEAMED OR DEEP-FRIED VEGETABLES SERVED WITH A DIPPING SAUCE ARE COMMON FARE THROUGHOUT SOUTH-EAST ASIA. IN VIETNAM, THEY ARE USUALLY SERVED WITH THE UBIQUITOUS NUOC CHAM, BUT CAN ALSO BE SERVED WITH A PEANUT OR GINGER DIPPING SAUCE.*

SERVES FOUR TO SIX

INGREDIENTS

6 eggs
1 long aubergine (eggplant), peeled, halved lengthways and sliced into half moons
1 long sweet potato, peeled and sliced into rounds
1 small butternut squash, peeled, seeded, halved lengthways and cut into half moons
salt and ground black pepper
vegetable oil, for deep-frying
*nuoc cham*, for dipping

**VARIATIONS**
Courgettes (zucchini), angled loofah, taro root or pumpkin could also be used.

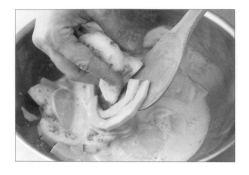

**1** Beat the eggs in a wide bowl. Season with salt and pepper. Toss the vegetables in the egg to coat thoroughly.

**2** Heat enough oil for deep-frying in a large wok. Cook the vegetables in small batches, making sure there is plenty of egg coating them.

**3** When they turn golden, lift them out of the oil with a slotted spoon and drain on kitchen paper.

**4** Keep them warm while the remaining vegetables are being fried. Serve warm with *nuoc cham* or a dipping sauce of your choice.

**Per portion** Energy 280Kcal/1164kJ; Protein 8; Carbohydrate 11.9g, of which sugars 5.7g; Fat 23g, of which saturates 4g; Cholesterol 190mg; Calcium 90mg; Fibre 3.5g; Sodium 84mg

# STIR-FRIED WATER SPINACH <u>WITH</u> NUOC CHAM

*IN THE VIETNAMESE COUNTRYSIDE THIS DISH IS A FAVOURITE WITH ROADSIDE VENDORS. ASPARAGUS AND CAULIFLOWER CAN ALSO BE STIR-FRIED IN A SIMILAR MANNER. SERVE ANY OF THESE VERSIONS AS A SIDE DISH TO MEAT OR FISH, OR WITH OTHER VEGETABLE DISHES.*

SERVES THREE TO FOUR

INGREDIENTS
   30ml/2 tbsp groundnut (peanut) oil
   2 garlic cloves, finely chopped
   2 red or green Thai chillies, seeded
    and finely chopped
   500g/1¼lb fresh water spinach
   45ml/3 tbsp *nuoc cham*
   salt and ground black pepper

**VARIATION**
Any type of greens would work, particularly ordinary spinach, although tough leaves should be blanched first.

**1** Heat a wok or large pan and add the oil. Stir in the garlic and chillies and stir-fry for 1 minute, then add the spinach and toss around the pan.

**2** Once the spinach leaves begin to wilt, add the *nuoc cham*, making sure it coats the spinach. Season to taste with salt and pepper and serve immediately.

**Per portion** Energy 120Kcal/500kJ; Protein 3g; Carbohydrate 5g, of which sugars 3g; Fat 10g, of which saturates 2g; Cholesterol 0mg; Calcium 36mg; Fibre 3.3g; Sodium 200mg

# CRISP-FRIED TOFU IN A TANGY TOMATO SAUCE

*THIS IS A LIGHT, TASTY VIETNAMESE DISH. THE BUDDHIST MONKS WHO ADHERE TO A VEGETARIAN DIET ENJOY IT TOO, SIMPLY BY REPLACING THE FISH SAUCE, NUOC MAM, WITH SOY SAUCE.*

**2** Reserve 30ml/2 tbsp oil in the wok. Add the shallots, chilli, ginger and garlic and stir-fry until fragrant. Stir in the tomatoes, *nuoc mam* and sugar. Reduce the heat and simmer for 10–15 minutes until it resembles a sauce. Stir in 105ml/ 7 tbsp water and bring to the boil.

**3** Season with a little pepper and return the tofu to the pan. Mix well and simmer gently for 2–3 minutes to heat through. Garnish with mint leaves and chilli strips and serve immediately.

SERVES FOUR

INGREDIENTS
  vegetable or groundnut (peanut) oil,
    for deep-frying
  450g/1lb firm tofu, rinsed and cut
    into bitesize cubes
  4 shallots, finely sliced
  1 Thai chilli, seeded and chopped
  25g/1oz fresh root ginger, peeled
    and finely chopped
  4 garlic cloves, finely chopped
  6 large ripe tomatoes, skinned,
    seeded and finely chopped
  30ml/2 tbsp *nuoc mam*
  10ml/2 tsp sugar
  mint leaves and strips of red chilli,
    to garnish
  ground black pepper

**1** Heat enough oil for deep-frying in a wok or heavy pan. Fry the tofu, in batches, until crisp and golden. Remove with a slotted spoon and drain on kitchen paper.

**COOK'S TIP**
This recipe is delicious as a side dish or as a main dish with noodles or rice.

**Per portion** Energy 234Kcal/974kJ; Protein 11g; Carbohydrate 11g, of which sugars 10.1g; Fat 16g, of which saturates 2g; Cholesterol 0mg; Calcium 619mg; Fibre 2.7g; Sodium 25mg

# SPICY TOFU WITH LEMON GRASS, BASIL AND PEANUTS

*IN VIETNAM, AROMATIC PEPPER LEAVES ARE OFTEN USED AS THE HERB ELEMENT BUT, BECAUSE THESE ARE QUITE DIFFICULT TO FIND OUTSIDE SOUTH-EAST ASIA, YOU CAN USE BASIL LEAVES INSTEAD.*

SERVES THREE TO FOUR

INGREDIENTS

3 lemon grass stalks, finely chopped
45ml/3 tbsp soy sauce
2 red Serrano chillies, seeded and
    finely chopped
2 garlic cloves, crushed
5ml/1 tsp ground turmeric
10ml/2 tsp sugar
300g/11oz tofu, rinsed, drained,
    patted dry and cut into
    bitesize cubes
30ml/2 tbsp groundnut (peanut) oil
45ml/3 tbsp roasted peanuts,
    chopped
1 bunch fresh basil, stalks removed
salt

1 In a bowl, mix together the lemon grass, soy sauce, chillies, garlic, turmeric and sugar until the sugar has dissolved. Add a little salt to taste and add the tofu, making sure it is well coated. Leave to marinate for 1 hour.

**VARIATION**
Lime, coriander (cilantro) or curry leaves would work well in this simple stir-fry.

2 Heat a wok or heavy pan. Pour in the oil, add the marinated tofu, and cook, stirring frequently, until it is golden brown on all sides. Add the peanuts and most of the basil leaves.

3 Divide the tofu among individual serving dishes, scatter the remaining basil leaves over the top and serve hot or at room temperature.

**Per portion** Energy 120Kcal/500kJ; Protein 3g; Carbohydrate 5g, of which sugars 3g; Fat 10g, of which saturates 2g; Cholesterol 0mg; Calcium 36mg; Fibre 3.3g; Sodium 200mg

# CHICKEN AND SHREDDED CABBAGE SALAD

*IN SOME VIETNAMESE HOUSEHOLDS, A WHOLE CHICKEN IS COOKED IN WATER WITH HERBS AND FLAVOURINGS TO MAKE A BROTH. THE CHICKEN IS THEN SHREDDED. SOME OF THE MEAT GOES BACK INTO THE BROTH, THE REST IS TOSSED IN THIS SALAD, POPULAR THROUGHOUT THE COUNTRY.*

SERVES FOUR TO SIX

INGREDIENTS
    450g/1lb chicken, cooked and torn
      into thin strips
    1 white Chinese cabbage, trimmed
      and finely shredded
    2 carrots, finely shredded or grated
    a small bunch fresh mint, stalks
      removed, finely shredded
    1 small bunch fresh coriander
      (cilantro) leaves, to garnish
For the dressing
    30ml/2 tbsp vegetable or groundnut
      (peanut) oil
    30ml/2 tbsp white rice vinegar

45ml/3 tbsp *nuoc mam* or *tuk trey*
juice of 2 limes
30ml/2 tbsp palm sugar
2 red Thai chillies, seeded and finely
  chopped
25g/1oz fresh young root ginger,
  sliced
3 garlic cloves, crushed
2 shallots, finely chopped

**1** First make the dressing. In a bowl, beat the oil, vinegar, *nuoc mam* or *tuk trey*, and lime juice with the sugar, until it has dissolved. Stir in the other ingredients and leave to stand for about 30 minutes to let the flavours mingle.

**2** Put the cooked chicken strips, cabbage, carrots and mint in a large bowl. Pour over the dressing and toss well. Garnish with coriander leaves and serve.

**Per portion** Energy 142Kcal/597kJ; Protein 19; Carbohydrate 5.7g, of which sugars 5.1g; Fat 4.8g, of which saturates 0.7g; Cholesterol 53mg; Calcium 53mg; Fibre 1.9g; Sodium 57mg

# FRIED SHALLOTS

*SHALLOTS FRIED WITH A COMBINATION OF GINGER, SPRING ONIONS AND GARLIC, OR JUST ONE OR TWO OF THESE FLAVOURINGS, LEND A CRUNCH AND A SWEETNESS TO FINISHED DISHES. SERVED AS GARNISHES OR CONDIMENTS, THEY ARE FOUND THROUGHOUT SOUTH-EAST ASIA.*

TO GARNISH THREE TO FOUR DISHES

INGREDIENTS

150ml/¼ pint/⅔ cup vegetable or groundnut (peanut) oil
6 shallots, halved lengthways and sliced along the grain
50g/2oz fresh root ginger, peeled and cut into fine strips
6 spring onions (scallions), trimmed, cut into 2.5cm/1in pieces and halved lengthways
3 garlic cloves, halved lengthways and cut into thin strips

**1** Heat the oil in a wok or small pan. Stir in the shallots, ginger, spring onions and garlic. Stir-fry until golden, but not brown. Remove with a slotted spoon and drain on kitchen paper.

**2** Leave to cool and store in a jar in the refrigerator for up to 1 week. Use as a garnish or put it on the table as a condiment. The leftover, flavoured oil can be used for stir-fries.

**Per portion** Energy 471Kcal/1942kJ; Protein 4g; Carbohydrate 14g, of which sugars 9g; Fat 44.7g, of which saturates 5.2g; Cholesterol 0mg; Calcium 77mg; Fibre 3.7g; Sodium 38mg

# SPRING ONION OIL

*MANY DISHES CALL FOR A FLAVOURED OIL TO BE DRIZZLED OVER NOODLES, OR BRUSHED ON GRILLED MEAT. IN VIETNAM, SPRING ONION OIL IS ALMOST ALWAYS AT HAND, READY TO BE SPLASHED INTO SOUPS, AND OVER MANY NOODLE AND STIR-FRIED DISHES.*

MAKES ABOUT 250ML/8FL OZ/1 CUP

INGREDIENTS
    250ml/8fl oz/1 cup vegetable or
        groundnut (peanut) oil
    15 spring onions (scallions), trimmed
        and finely sliced

**COOK'S TIP**
It is important not to fry the spring onions for too long: they should be golden and sweet. If they become dark brown, they will have a bitter taste. Many South-east Asian cooks prepare batches of this garnish to keep at hand for the week's cooking. Refrigerate after making up a batch. They will keep for 2 weeks.

**1** Heat the oil, stir in the spring onions and fry until golden. Pour the oil into a heatproof jug (pitcher) and leave to cool.

**2** Pour the oil into a glass bottle or jar, seal tightly, and store in a cool place.

**Per portion** Energy 1698Kcal/6985kJ; Protein 3g; Carbohydrate 4g, of which sugars 4g; Fat 186g, of which saturates 22g; Cholesterol 0mg; Calcium 59mg; Fibre 2.3g; Sodium 11mg

# NUOC LEO

*THIS HOT PEANUT DIPPING SAUCE IS POPULAR THROUGHOUT VIETNAM. ADJUST THE PROPORTIONS OF CHILLI, SUGAR OR LIQUID, ADDING MORE OR LESS ACCORDING TO TASTE. THIS IS ESPECIALLY GOOD SERVED WITH STEAMED, STIR-FRIED OR DEEP-FRIED VEGETABLES.*

MAKES ABOUT 300ML/10FL OZ/2¼ CUPS

INGREDIENTS
    15ml/1 tbsp vegetable oil
    2 garlic cloves, finely chopped
    2 red Thai chillies, seeded
     and chopped
    115g/4oz/⅔ cup unsalted roasted
     peanuts, finely chopped
    150ml/¼ pint/⅔ cup chicken stock
    60ml/4 tbsp coconut milk
    15ml/1 tbsp hoisin sauce
    15ml/1 tbsp *nuoc mam*
    15ml/1 tbsp sugar

**1** Heat the oil in a small wok and stir in the garlic and chillies. Stir-fry until they begin to colour, then add all but 15ml/ 1 tbsp of the peanuts. Stir-fry for a few minutes until the oil from the peanuts begins to weep. Add the remaining ingredients and bring to the boil.

**COOK'S TIP**
If you don't use it in one sitting, this sauce will keep in the refrigerator for about one week.

**2** Simmer until the sauce thickens and oil appears on the surface.

**3** Transfer the sauce to a serving dish and garnish with the reserved peanuts.

**Per portion** Energy 848Kcal/3525kJ; Protein 31g; Carbohydrate 39g, of which sugars 31g; Fat 64g, of which saturates 11g; Cholesterol 0mg; Calcium 104mg; Fibre 8g; Sodium 2498mg

# NUOC CHAM

*THERE ARE MANY VERSIONS OF THIS POPULAR CHILLI DIPPING SAUCE, VARYING IN DEGREES OF SWEETNESS, SOURNESS AND HEAT. SOME PEOPLE ADD RICE VINEGAR TO THE MIX.*

MAKES ABOUT 200ML/7FL OZ/SCANT 1 CUP

INGREDIENTS
    4 garlic cloves, roughly chopped
    2 red Thai chillies, seeded and
     roughly chopped
    15ml/1 tbsp sugar
    juice of 1 lime
    60ml/4 tbsp *nuoc mam*

**1** Using a mortar and pestle, pound the garlic with the chillies and sugar and grind to make a paste.

**2** Squeeze in the lime juice, add the *nuoc mam* and then stir in 60–75ml/ 4–5 tbsp water to taste. Blend well.

**Per portion** Energy 140Kcal/593kJ; Protein 5.; Carbohydrate 30g, of which sugars 24g; Fat 0.4g, of which saturates 0.1g; Cholesterol 0mg; Calcium 30mg; Fibre 2.4g; Sodium 4277mg

# SWEET SNACKS & DRINKS

*Juicy fruit and sweet snacks are enjoyed by all Vietnamese. Rather than being served at the end of a meal, sweet snacks tend to be devoured on a whim. Ripe fruit is peeled and eaten, made into a fruit salad or crushed into juice; ice cream is made with exotic flavours such as star anise; and hot, sweet soups or refreshing drinks are prepared with fruit or sweetened beans, such as Rainbow Drink, made with mung beans, azuki beans, coconut milk and crushed ice.*

# VIETNAMESE FRIED BANANAS

*WHEREVER YOU GO IN VIETNAM, YOU WILL FIND FRIED BANANAS. THEY ARE EATEN HOT, STRAIGHT FROM THE PAN, AS A QUICK AND TASTY SNACK. FOR A MORE INDULGENT TREAT, THEY MIGHT BE COMBINED WITH ONE OF THE LOVELY FRENCH-STYLE ICE CREAMS.*

SERVES FOUR

INGREDIENTS
  4 ripe but firm bananas
  vegetable oil, for deep-frying
  caster (superfine) sugar, for sprinkling
For the batter
  115g/4oz/1 cup rice flour or plain
    (all-purpose) flour
  2.5ml/½ tsp baking powder
  45ml/3 tbsp caster (superfine) sugar
  150ml/¼ pint/⅔ cup water
  150ml/¼ pint/⅔ cup beer

**1** To make the batter, sift the flour with the baking powder into a bowl. Add the sugar and beat in a little of the water and beer to make a smooth paste. Gradually beat in the rest of the water and beer to form a thick batter. Leave to stand for 20 minutes.

**2** Peel the bananas and cut them in half crossways, then in half again lengthways. Heat enough vegetable oil for deep-frying in a wok or a large, heavy pan.

**3** Cook the bananas in batches, so they don't stick together in the pan. Dip each one into the beer batter, making sure it is well coated, and carefully slip it into the hot oil. Use tongs or chopsticks for turning and make sure each piece is crisp and golden all over.

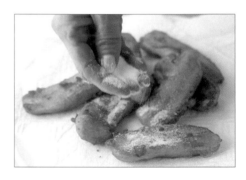

**4** Drain the fried bananas on kitchen paper and sprinkle them with sugar. Serve immediately and eat hot.

Per portion Energy 290Kcal/1211kJ; Protein 3g; Carbohydrate 48g, of which sugars 22g; Fat 9g, of which saturates 1g; Cholesterol 0mg; Calcium 22mg; Fibre 1.7g; Sodium 600mg

# JUNGLE FRUITS IN LEMON GRASS SYRUP

*THIS EXOTIC AND REFRESHING FRUIT SALAD CAN BE MADE WITH ANY COMBINATION OF TROPICAL FRUITS — JUST GO FOR A GOOD BALANCE OF COLOUR, FLAVOUR AND TEXTURE. YOU CAN ALSO FLAVOUR THE SYRUP WITH GINGER RATHER THAN LEMON GRASS, IF YOU PREFER.*

SERVES SIX

INGREDIENTS

   1 firm papaya
   1 small pineapple
   2 small star fruit, sliced into stars
   12 fresh lychees, peeled and stoned
    (pitted) or 14oz/400g can lychees
   2 firm yellow or green bananas, peeled
    and cut diagonally into slices
   mint leaves, to decorate
For the syrup
   115g/4oz/generous ½ cup caster
    (superfine) sugar
   2 lemon grass stalks, bruised and
    halved lengthways

**1** To make the syrup, put 225ml/ 7½ fl oz/1 cup water into a heavy pan with the sugar and lemon grass stalks. Bring to the boil, stirring constantly until the sugar has dissolved, then reduce the heat and simmer for 15 minutes. Leave to cool.

**2** Peel and halve the papaya, remove the seeds and slice the flesh crossways. Peel the pineapple and slice it into rounds. Remove the core and cut each round in half. (Keep the core and slice it for a stir-fry.)

**3** Put all the fruit into a bowl. Pour the syrup, including the lemon grass stalks, over the top and toss to combine. Cover and chill for 6 hours, or overnight. Before serving, remove the lemon grass stalks and decorate with mint leaves.

**Per portion** Energy 160Kcal/683kJ; Protein 1g; Carbohydrate 41g, of which sugars 40g; Fat 0g, of which saturates 0g; Cholesterol 0mg; Calcium 22mg; Fibre 1.8g; Sodium 0mg

# DEEP-FRIED MUNG BEAN DUMPLINGS

*Sweet and savoury rice dumplings are popular snacks in Vietnam. In this dish, dau xanh vung, the potato and rice-flour dumplings are stuffed with the classic Vietnamese filling of sweetened mung bean paste and then rolled in sesame seeds.*

**3** In a large bowl, beat the flours and remaining sugar into the mashed potato. Add about 200ml/7fl oz/scant 1 cup water to bind the mixture into a moist dough. Divide the dough into 24 pieces, roll each one into a small ball, then flatten with the heel of your hand to make a disc and lay out on a lightly floured board.

**4** Divide the mung bean paste into 24 small portions. Place one portion of mung bean paste in the centre of a dough disc. Fold over the edges of the dough and then shape into a ball. Repeat for the remaining dumplings.

**5** Spread the sesame seeds on a plate and roll the dumplings in them until evenly coated. Heat enough oil for deep-frying in a wok or heavy pan. Fry the balls in batches until golden. Drain on kitchen paper and serve warm.

**VARIATION**
These little fried dumplings may also be filled with a sweetened red bean paste, sweetened taro root or, as in China, a lotus paste.

SERVES SIX

INGREDIENTS
  100g/3½oz/scant ½ cup split
    mung beans, soaked for 6 hours
    and drained
  115g/4oz/generous ½ cup caster
    (superfine) sugar
  300g/10½oz/scant 3 cups glutinous
    rice flour
  50g/2oz/½ cup rice flour
  1 medium potato, boiled in its skin,
    peeled and mashed
  75g/3oz/6 tbsp sesame seeds
  vegetable oil, for deep-frying

**1** Put the mung beans in a large pan with half the caster sugar and pour in 450ml/¾ pint/scant 2 cups water. Bring to the boil, stirring constantly until all the sugar has dissolved. Reduce the heat and simmer gently for 15–20 minutes until the mung beans are soft. You may need to add more water if the beans are becoming dry, otherwise they will burn on the bottom of the pan.

**2** Once the mung beans are soft and all the water has been absorbed, reduce the beans to a smooth paste in a mortar and pestle or food processor and cool.

**Per portion** Energy 321Kcal/1346kJ; Protein 7g; Carbohydrate 40g, of which sugars 21g; Fat 16g, of which saturates 2g; Cholesterol 0mg; Calcium 104mg; Fibre 3.1g; Sodium 0mg

# TAPIOCA WITH BANANA AND COCONUT

*THIS IS THE TYPE OF POPULAR DESSERT THAT EVERYBODY'S MOTHER OR GRANDMOTHER REGULARLY MAKES IN VIETNAM. SWEET AND NOURISHING, IT IS MADE WITH TAPIOCA PEARLS COOKED IN COCONUT MILK AND SWEETENED WITH BANANAS AND SUGAR.*

SERVES FOUR

INGREDIENTS
550ml/18fl oz/2½ cups water
40g/1½oz tapioca pearls
550ml/18fl oz/2½ cups coconut milk
90g/3½oz/½ cup sugar
3 ripe bananas, diced
salt

**COOK'S TIP**
A pinch of salt added to this recipe enhances the flavour of the coconut milk and counterbalances the sweetness. You can try the recipe with sweet potato, taro root, yellow corn or rice.

**1** Pour the water into a pan and bring it to the boil. Stir in the tapioca pearls, reduce the heat and simmer for about 20 minutes, until translucent. Add the coconut milk, sugar and a pinch of salt. Cook gently for 30 minutes.

**2** Stir in the diced bananas and cook them for 5–10 minutes until soft. Spoon into individual warmed bowls and serve immediately.

**Per portion** Energy 226Kcal/964kJ; Protein 1.5g; Carbohydrate 57.2g, of which sugars 45.9g; Fat 0.7g, of which saturates 0.4g; Cholesterol 0mg; Calcium 57mg; Fibre 0.9g; Sodium 154mg.

# COCONUT CRÈME CARAMEL

*BASED ON THE CLASSIC FRENCH DESSERT, THIS VIETNAMESE VERSION IS MADE WITH COCONUT MILK. POPULAR THROUGHOUT VIETNAM, IT IS SERVED BOTH AS A SNACK AND AS A DESSERT IN RESTAURANTS, WHERE IT IS SOMETIMES GARNISHED WITH MINT LEAVES.*

SERVES FOUR TO SIX

INGREDIENTS
    4 large (US extra large) eggs
    4 egg yolks
    50g/2oz/¼ cup caster (superfine)
      sugar
    600ml/1 pint/2½ cups coconut
      milk
    toasted slivers of coconut,
      to decorate
For the caramel
    150g/5oz/¾ cup caster (superfine)
      sugar

**1** Preheat the oven to 160°C/325°F/ Gas 3. To make the caramel, heat the sugar and 75ml/5 tbsp water in a heavy pan, stirring constantly until the sugar dissolves. Bring to the boil and, without stirring, let the mixture bubble until it is dark golden and almost like treacle.

**2** Pour the caramel into an ovenproof dish, tilting the dish to swirl it around so that it covers the bottom and sides – you will need to do this quickly. Put the dish aside and leave the caramel to set.

**3** In a bowl, beat the eggs and egg yolks with the caster sugar. Heat the coconut milk in a small pan, but don't allow it to boil. Then gradually pour it on to the egg mixture, while beating constantly. Pour the mixture through a sieve (strainer) over the caramel in the dish or individual ramekins.

**4** Set the dish or ramekins in a bain-marie. You can use a roasting pan or wide oven dish half-filled with water. Place it in the oven for about 50 minutes, or until the custard has just set, but still feels soft when touched with the fingertips. Leave the dish to cool, then chill in the refrigerator for at least 6 hours, or overnight.

**COOK'S TIP**
• You can use this recipe to make six small individual desserts using ramekin dishes instead of a large dish.

**VARIATION**
• If you are not keen on coconut, you can use full-fat fresh milk instead of coconut milk and infuse it with a vanilla pod, orange peel or aniseed.

**5** To serve, loosen the custard around the sides using a thin, sharp knife. Place a flat serving plate over the top and invert the custard, holding on to the dish and plate at the same time. Shake it a little before removing the inverted dish, then carefully lift it off as the caramel drizzles down the sides and forms a puddle around the pudding.

**6** Decorate the custard with fresh grated coconut and mint leaves, and serve.

**VARIATION**
For an alternative garnish, try toasted coconut or make a small batch of sugar syrup with finely shredded ginger or orange peel.

**Per portion** Energy 256Kcal/1078kJ; Protein 9g; Carbohydrate 31g, of which sugars 31g; Fat 11g, of which saturates 4g; Cholesterol 338mg; Calcium 79mg; Fibre 0.4g; Sodium 200mg

# STAR ANISE ICE CREAM

*THIS SYRUP-BASED ICE CREAM IS FLAVOURED WITH THE CLEAN, WARMING LICORICE TASTE OF STAR ANISE AND WILL PUNCTUATE THE END OF A SPICY VIETNAMESE MEAL PERFECTLY, LEAVING YOU WITH A REALLY EXOTIC TASTE IN YOUR MOUTH. GROUND STAR ANISE IS ALSO USED TO DECORATE THE FINAL DISH.*

SERVES SIX TO EIGHT

INGREDIENTS
  500ml/17fl oz/2¼ cups double
    (heavy) cream
  8 whole star anise
  90g/3½oz/½ cup caster (superfine)
    sugar
  4 large (US extra large) egg yolks
  ground star anise, to decorate

**1** In a heavy pan, heat the cream with the star anise to just below boiling point, then remove from the heat and leave to infuse until cool.

**COOK'S TIP**
Spices play an important role in the ice creams from the south of Vietnam, with their lively tastes of cinnamon, clove, star anise and pandanus leaf. This ice cream is often served as a palate cleanser.

**2** In another pan, dissolve the sugar in 150ml/¼ pint/⅔ cup water, stirring constantly. Bring to the boil for a few minutes to form a light syrup, then leave to cool for 1 minute.

**3** Whisk the egg yolks in a bowl. Trickle in the hot syrup, whisking constantly, until the mixture becomes mousse-like. Pour in the infused cream through a sieve (strainer), and continue to whisk.

**4** Pour the mixture into an ice cream maker and churn until frozen. Alternatively, pour the mixture into a freezerproof container and freeze for 4 hours, beating twice with a fork or whisking with an electric mixer to break up the ice crystals. To serve, dust with a little ground star anise.

**Per portion** Energy 393Kcal/1623kJ; Protein 3g; Carbohydrate 14g, of which sugars 14g; Fat 37g, of which saturates 22g; Cholesterol 198mg; Calcium 45mg; Fibre 0g; Sodium 10mg

# RAINBOW DRINK

*THIRST-QUENCHING AND APPETIZING AT THE SAME TIME, RAINBOW DRINKS ARE A DELIGHTFUL SOUTH-EAST ASIAN TREAT. TWO KINDS OF SWEETENED BEANS ARE COLOURFULLY LAYERED WITH CRUSHED ICE, DRENCHED IN COCONUT MILK AND TOPPED WITH JELLIED AGAR AGAR.*

SERVES FOUR

INGREDIENTS

50g/2oz dried split mung beans, soaked for 4 hours and drained
50g/2oz red azuki beans, soaked for 4 hours and drained
25g/1oz/2 tbsp sugar

For the syrup

300ml/½ pint/1¼ cups coconut milk
50g/2oz/¼ cup sugar
25g/1oz tapioca pearls
crushed ice, to serve
15g/½oz jellied agar agar, soaked in warm water for 30 minutes and shredded into long strands, to decorate

**2** In a heavy pan, bring the coconut milk to the boil. Reduce the heat and stir in the sugar, until it dissolves. Add the tapioca pearls and simmer for about 10 minutes, until they become transparent. Leave to cool and chill in the refrigerator.

**3** Divide the beans among four tall glasses, add a layer of crushed ice, then the azuki beans and more ice. Pour the coconut syrup over the top and decorate with strands of agar agar. Serve immediately with straws and long spoons.

**1** Put the mung beans and azuki beans into two separate pans with 15g/l/½oz/ 1 tbsp sugar each. Pour in enough water to cover and, stirring all the time, bring it to the boil. Reduce the heat and leave both pans to simmer for about 15 minutes, stirring from time to time, until the beans are tender but not mushy – you may have to add more water. Drain the beans, leave to cool and chill separately in the refrigerator.

**COOK'S TIP**

Many variations of rainbow drinks are served throughout South-east Asia, some combining ingredients such as lotus seeds, taro, sweet potato, and tapioca pearls with exotic fruits. Served in tall, clear glasses in the markets, restaurants and bars they are popular in both Vietnam and Cambodia.

**Per portion** Energy 188Kcal/800kJ; Protein 6g; Carbohydrate 42g, of which sugars 25g; Fat 0.5g, of which saturates 0.2g; Cholesterol 0mg; Calcium 55mg; Fibre 2.5g; Sodium 87mg

# SHOPPING INFORMATION

## AUSTRALIA
Asian Supermarkets Pty Ltd
116 Charters Towers Road
Townsville QLD 4810
Tel: (07) 4772 3997

Duc Hung Long Asian
　Foodstore
95 The Crescent
Fairfield NSW 2165
Tel: (02) 9728 1092

Kongs Trading Pty Ltd
8 Kingscote Street
Kewdale WA 6105
Tel: (08) 9353 3380

Saigon Asian Food Retail
6 Cape Street
Dickson ACT 2602
Tel: (02) 6247 4251

The Spice and Herb Asian Shop
200 Old Cleveland Road
Capalaba QLD 4157
Tel: (07) 3245 5300

Sydney Fish Market Pty Ltd
Cnr Pyrmont Bridge Road and
　Bank Street
Pyrmont NSW 2009
Tel: (02) 9660 1611

Burlington Supermarkets
Chinatown Mall
Fortitude Valley QLD 4006
Tel: (07) 3216 1828

## CANADA
Dahl's Oriental Food
822 Broadview
Toronto, Ontario M4K 2P7
Tel: (416) 463-8109

Hong Kong Emporium
364 Young Street,
Toronto
Ontario M5B 1S5
Tel: (416) 977-3386

## SOUTH AFRICA
Akhalwaya and Sons
Gillies Street, Burgersdorp
Johannesburg
Tel: (11) 838-1008

Kashmiri Spice Centre
95 Church Street
Mayfair, Johannesburg
Tel: (11)839-3883

Haribak and Sons Ltd
31 Pine Street
Durban
Tel: (31) 32-662

## UNITED KINGDOM
Golden Gate Supermarket
16 Newport Place
London WC2H 7JS
Tel: 020 7437 6266

Loon Fung Supermarket
42–44 Gerrard Street
London W1V 7LP
Tel: 020 7437 7332

Rum Wong Supermarket
London Road
Guildford GU1 2AF
Tel: 01483 451568

Wing Tai
11a Aylesham Centre
Rye Lane
London SE15 5EW
Tel: 020 7635 0714

Wing Yip
395 Edgware Road
London NW2 6LN
Tel: 020 7450 0422
*also at*
Oldham Road
Ancoats
Manchester M4 5HU
Tel: 0161 832 3215
*and*
375 Nechells Park Road
Nechells
Birmingham B7 5NT
Tel: 0121 327 3838

**Mail Order Companies**
Fiddes Payne Herbs and
　Spices Ltd
Unit 3B, Thorpe Way, Banbury
Oxfordshire OX16 8XL
Tel: 01295 253 888

Seasoned Pioneers Ltd
101 Summers Road
Brunswick Business Park
Liverpool L3 4BJ
Tel: 0151 709 9330
www.seasonedpioneers.com

## UNITED STATES
Asian Food Market
6450 Market Street
Upper Darby, PA 19082
Tel: (610) 352-4433

Asian Foods Ltd.
260–280 West Lehigh Avenue
Philadelphia, PA 19133
Tel: (215) 291-9500

Asian Market
2513 Stewart Avenue
Las Vegas, NV 89101
Tel: (702) 387-3373

Asian Market
18815 Eureka Road
South Gate, MI 48195
Fax: (734) 246-4795

Augusta Market Oriental Foods
2117 Martin Luther King Jr.
　Boulevard
Atlanta, GA 30901
Tel: (706) 722-4988

Bangkok Market
4757 Melrose Avenue
Los Angeles, CA 90029
Tel: (203) 662-7990

Bharati Food & Spice Center
6163 Reynolds Road Suite G
Morrow, GA 30340
Tel: (770) 961-9007

First Asian Food Center
3420 East Ponce De Leon Ave
Scottsdale, GA 30079
Tel: (404) 292-6508

Huy Fong Foods Inc.
5001 Earle Avenue
Rosemead, CA 91770
Tel: (626) 286-8328

Khanh Tam Oriental Market
4051 Buford Highway NE
Atlanta, GA 30345
Tel: (404) 728-0393

Oriental Grocery
11827 Del Amo Boulevard
Cerritos, CA 90701
Tel: (310) 924-1029

Oriental Market
670 Central Park Avenue
Yonkers, NY 10013
Tel: (212) 349-1979

The Oriental Pantry
423 Great Road
Acton, MA 01720
Tel: (978) 264-4576

Saigon Asian Market
10090 Central Avenue
Biloxi, MS 39532
Tel: (228) 392-8044

# INDEX

## AUTHOR'S ACKNOWLEDGEMENTS

In a book of this nature, there is always a great deal of research.
For this I must mention the *Essentials of Asian Cuisine* by Corinne
Trang, the most informative book on culinary cultures of South-east
Asia; *South East Asian Food* by Rosemary Brissenden; *Authentic
Vietnamese Cooking* by Corinne Trang, *A Vietnamese Feast* by Andy
Lee; and the excellent *Rough Guide to Vietnam*. On the ground, I
would like to say a big thank you to Douglas Toidy and Le Huong at
their Vung Tau fish farm, and to Peter Grant at Frank's, Singapore.
And, I would like to thank the team at Anness Publishing Ltd.

## PUBLISHER'S ACKNOWLEDGEMENTS

The publisher would like to thank Martin Brigdale for his
photography shown throughout the book, with the exception of
the following images:
t = top; b = bottom; r = right; l = left
Alamy page 9br (E J Baumeister Jr)
Robert Harding Picture Library pages 6tr, 6bl, 8t
Superstock Ltd page 9tr